338.9415

Items should be returned on or before the last date shown below. Items not already requested by other borrowers may be renewed in person, in writing or by telephone. To renew, please quote the number on the barcode label. To renew online a PIN is required. This can be requested at your local library. Renew online @ **www.dublincitypubliclibraries.ie** Fines charged for overdue items will include postage incurred in recovery. Damage to or loss of items will be charged to the borrower.

Leabharlanna Poiblí Chathair Bhaile Átha Cliath
Dublin City Public Libraries

Baile Átha Cliath
Dublin City

Brainse Rátheanaigh
Raheny Branch
Tel: 8315521

Date Due	Date Due	Date Due
- 1 MAR 2014 10/6/2014		

D1355544

About the Authors

Finbarr D. Bradley

Finbarr D. Bradley teaches at University College Dublin (UCD). He has been a professor at both Dublin City University (DCU) and the National University of Ireland (NUI), Maynooth, and a visiting professor at the University of Michigan, Fordham University and Aalto University. He co-authored with James J. Kennelly the 2008 book, *Capitalising on Culture, Competing on Difference* (Blackhall Publishing), co-edited a book of essays on Ireland's economic crisis based on the 2009 MacGill Summer School and wrote the 2011 monograph *Meon Gaelach, Aigne Nualaíoch* (Coiscéim). He holds an engineering degree from University College Cork (UCC) and a PhD in International Business/Finance from the Stern School of Business, New York University (NYU).

James J. Kennelly

James J. Kennelly is Professor of International Business at Skidmore College, Saratoga Springs, New York. He has been a Visiting Professor at NYU's Stern School of Business and at Aalto University. His book *The Kerry Way: A History of the Kerry Group* was published by Oak Tree Press in 2001. His 2008 co-authored book (with Finbarr Bradley), *Capitalising on Culture, Competing on Difference* (Blackhall Publishing) focused upon Ireland's efforts to develop in a manner that is economically, socially and environmentally sustainable. He holds an accounting degree from Montclair State University, New Jersey and a PhD in International Business/Management from the Stern School of Business, NYU.

ii

The Irish Edge

How Enterprises Compete on
Authenticity and Place

Finbarr D. Bradley and James J. Kennelly

ORPEN PRESS

Orpen Press
Lonsdale House
Avoca Avenue
Blackrock
Co. Dublin
Ireland

e-mail: info@orpenpress.com
www.orpenpress.com

Paperback ISBN: 978-1-909518-00-1
ePub ISBN: 978-1-909895-04-1
Kindle ISBN: 978-1-909895-03-4

Printed in Ireland by SPRINT-print Ltd.

Ireland must be re-created from within. The main work must be done in Ireland, and the centre of interest must be Ireland. When Irishmen realise this truth, the splendid human power of their country, so much of which now runs idly or disastrously to waste, will be utilised; and we may then look with confidence for the foundation of a fabric of Irish prosperity, framed in constructive thought, and laid enduringly in human character.
Horace Plunkett, Irish co-operator and reformer, 1904[1]

Acknowledgements

We would like to thank, first of all, our contacts at the enterprises profiled in this book, especially those entrepreneurs and organisational professionals who generously gave of their time and expertise in relating to us their inspiring stories. In particular, we would like to thank David Cox, Paul Cummins, Marie-Thérèse de Blacam, Ruairí de Blacam, Tarlach de Blacam, Brian de Staic, Mary Hawkes-Greene, Frank Hayes, Philip King, Dominique Lieb, Jamie McCarthy-Fisher, Malachy McCloskey, Louis Mulcahy, Tom O'Rahilly, Mícheál Ó Súilleabháin, Dearbhaill Standún, Charlie Troy, John Teeling and Mark Walton.

Friends and colleagues Frank Allen, John Fanning, Una FitzGibbon, Alexandra Gillies, Tomás Hardiman and Susan Ní Dhubhlaoich read sections or early drafts of the book (and there were many) and offered very useful insights and recommendations. Although we alone are responsible for any errors, our ideas were sharpened and the book was much improved by virtue of their generous help. *Buíochas le Donla uí Bhraonáin as comhairle Ghaeilge.*

At Orpen Press, we would like to thank Jennifer Thompson for her outstanding editorial work, her thoughtful and incisive advice on the manuscript, and her yeoman's work in helping us bring the manuscript to completion. It was a pleasure to work with her. We would also like to thank Eileen O'Brien for her patience and diligence in overseeing the creation of the cover, and Gerard O'Connor and Elizabeth Brennan for believing in this project and for their oversight of the endeavour.

Acknowledgements

Jim Kennelly would like to thank Skidmore College for a faculty development grant awarded for travel to Ireland in support of this research, and for giving him a home amongst a community of scholars for so many years. He would also like to thank all of his colleagues in the Department of Management and Business for their support and collegiality. Surprising as it may be to some authors, daily life does not stop just because a book is being pondered, planned, researched or written. We would both like to thank our families and friends for their support. Jim thanks his wife Linda and sons Brendan and Terence for their love and understanding. *Níl aon tinteán mar do thinteán féin.* He'd also like to thank his friend and co-author Finbarr Bradley for his unflagging enthusiasm and dedication to the ideas that are presented in this book, and his love for the culture, music and first national language of Ireland. He is one of a kind.

Ba mhaith le Fionnbarra buíochas faoi leith a ghabháil lena mhuintir, a dheartháir Diarmuid agus a dheirfiúracha Clár, Siobhán agus Emer. Gabhann sé buíochas ó chroí lena leathbhádóir Jim Kennelly. Ábhar inspioráide dó thar na blianta é an grá a léiríonn Jim do thír dhúchais a mhuintire.

Finbarr D. Bradley

I gcuimhne m'athar Mícheál, mo mháthar Máiréad agus mo mhuintir go léir atá anois ar shlí na fírinne. Suaimhneas síoraí dóibh.

James J. Kennelly

Do Linda, Brendan agus Terence, agus do mo mhuintir go léir, san am i láthair is am atá thart, i gcéin is i gcóngar.

Table of Contents

Table of Contents

Preface

Walk on air against your better judgement.
Seamus Heaney, Irish Nobel Prize winner, 1995[2]

If we had exercised our better judgement, we would perhaps never have written this book. It treads a path at variance with the economic orthodoxy that now holds sway in Ireland. But, at a time when Irish public policy remains focused upon foreign direct investment as the primary engine, if not the saviour, of the Irish economy, it troubles us that the accomplishments of successful, home-grown enterprises that are intimately rooted in both the soil and culture of Ireland are often overlooked or dismissed out of hand – treated as one-off curiosities or small enterprises that are 'not scalable' and, thus, not worthy of serious attention. This attitude towards indigenous enterprises that are uniquely distinguished by authenticity and integrity, by 'Irishness', reminds us of the counsel of Taoiseach Seán Lemass, the original architect of Ireland's outward-looking economic policy. Even as he was leading the country out of economic isolation into a tumultuous new world of international trade and investment, he cautioned:

❙❙ The people of the world will respect us only to the extent
that we respect ourselves, our history, our traditions, our
culture and our language ... it is all the more important
that we should preserve and develop every characteristic and value which distinguishes us from other nations.
The movement of the Irish people which brought us so

far on the road to independent nationhood was never inspired by materialistic motives alone. If it had been, it would have failed, and we in our day will fail also unless we recognise and utilise the spiritual forces which activate both men [*sic*] and nations.

Seán Lemass, former Taoiseach, 1961[3] 〃

We go even further: it is precisely these 'characteristics and values' which underlie significant, inimitable and very real competitive advantages for Irish enterprises that are based on culture, authenticity and a sense of place. After all, it is difference, not sameness, that matters in global markets – alas, a fact scarcely appreciated in contemporary Ireland.

As Ireland searches for the right mix of policies that will enable it to overcome its serious economic challenges, it has often failed to notice that at least part of the answer is right under its nose, hiding in plain sight. We believe that an economy is only successful when it serves the needs of the people and society in which it is embedded, and not the other way around. Indigenous Irish enterprises characterised by distinctiveness and authenticity must play a key role in a balanced development strategy that is financially, socially and environmentally sustainable. The best of these enterprises create 'shared value': creating social value whilst competing successfully with the best firms in the world. This is not just pie-in-the-sky thinking; such distinctiveness is already exemplified in any number of Irish enterprises that, even in the midst of economic recession, have built competitive, world-class businesses. These enterprises, Ireland-based and locally owned, demonstrate what we call the 'Irish edge'. Their stories are instructive and deserve to be told.

We have written this book, not to propose a detailed set of policy instructions, but to relate stories of successful firms that build upon Ireland's distinct cultural, human and natural resources. Such enterprises are essential to build not only the 'smart economy' but, ultimately, a successful, vigorous and diverse society and nation – one that is no less globally competitive for being distinctively Irish. In a time of no little doom and gloom, there are good stories out there! Some are truly inspiring.

Although we are business academicians by training, this book, whatever its faults, does not suffer from a narrow, disciplinary perspective. We have instead taken a broad interdisciplinary approach, for the themes that we examine demand no less. To that end, we hope that this book is of interest to policymakers, entrepreneurs and other business professionals, as well as the general reader with an interest in Ireland. Like our last book[4], the emphasis is on the Republic more than Northern Ireland, but we hope our ideas apply to the island as a whole.

If any reader has queries or comments on this work, please contact Orpen Press at info@orpenpress.com.

Finbarr D. Bradley, Blackrock, Co. Dublin
James J. Kennelly, Saratoga Springs, New York
July 2013

I

Ireland – Old and New

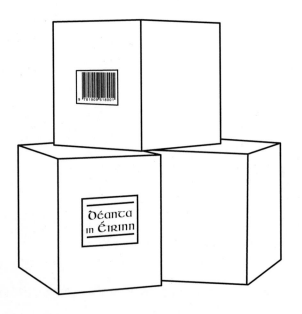

Déanta in Éirinn

1

Inis Meáin

*The thing that hugely influenced me was the older people here
– their independence and their self-sufficiency. The fact that
you've got to make do with what you've got because you're on an
island, and that's been my inspiration – always talking to the old
women who worked at home making sweaters for their husbands
and for the whole family.*

Tarlach de Blacam, entrepreneur, 2011[1]

This book tells the stories of Irish enterprises that have
successfully integrated their Irishness with the demands of
the global marketplace. They have done so by competing not
only on the basis of identity, but by adapting themselves to
what is called the *experience economy*. While we discuss the
idea of an experience economy in detail in Chapter 2, suffice
it to say here that in this the predominant economic offering is an 'experience'. The demand for personalised and
unique experiences has grown out of informed, connected,
empowered and active consumers weary of globalised,
mass-produced goods. Building on culture, tradition,
place, identity, language and sustainability, the enterprises
profiled in this book have developed unique products that
are distinctively Irish and offer experiences that are palpably
authentic. They are enterprises with integrity, innovating
and integrating the old and the new, creating products and
experiences based on traditional knowledge and distinctive

local resources. Such creativity fosters surprise: old pleasures designed, packaged and combined in novel ways and found in unexpected places.

Introducing Inis Meáin

One enterprise, Inis Meáin, sets the standard for our core thesis and provides an introduction to our book. A recent piece in the *Financial Times* profiling Inis Meáin was headlined 'A Chic Knitwear Outpost in the Aran Islands.'[2] Despite being labelled as 'Europe's most remote shopping destination', Inis Meáin has emerged as one of the most significant knitwear companies in the world.[3] Operating out of tiny Inis Meáin, the smallest of the Aran Islands (3 miles wide with a population of one hundred and sixty), it is recognised worldwide for upscale collections of jackets, shirts, sweaters and knitwear. Clothing bearing its distinctive logo – an upturned currach – is exported to exclusive stores and boutiques around the world.[4] These include Barneys and Bergdorf Goodman in New York, Grey Flannel in London, Isetan Mitsukoshi and United Arrows in Tokyo, Richetti in Parma, and 14 oz. in Berlin.

However, as visitors stand in the company's whitewashed showroom, with its floor-to-ceiling windows opening on inspiring views of the Atlantic and shelves stocked with sophisticated cashmere, merino and alpaca knits, it would behove them to remember that like many entrepreneurial ventures, it did not start out this way. On its founding in the mid-1970s, Tarlach de Blacam and his wife, Áine, executed a simpler business plan.

After graduating university, Tarlach spent a year in Dublin conducting research on place names but found his interests moving to community development. He first went to Inis Meáin in 1973 to study Irish. Shortly after moving back to Dublin, he met Áine, originally from Inis Meáin but teaching in Dublin. In 1976, they returned to the island together to set up the knitwear business. Drawing on the islanders' tradition of hand-knitting, Inis Meáin originally catered primarily to the tourist trade with a line of traditional Aran sweaters. Over the next few decades the company evolved into a sophisticated and successful, if small, world-class enterprise.

What makes Inis Meáin's clothing so authentic and distinctive is that its designs and manufacturing methods draw on traditional styles, colours and skills developed over centuries. Traditional fishermen's garments, first knitted by women of the island, offer inspiration to the de Blacams, who re-design and update these ancient classics. They refine and reinterpret local tradition for each of the company's collections in luxurious yarns. Irish place names on the island, translated as 'The Tomb of the Red-Haired Person', for example, or 'The Church of the Golden Hair', attest to the islanders' love of colours. The company's designs, inspired by the land, the surrounding sea and the changing seasons, illustrate these bright and subtle colours. Families on the island also often had their own distinctive patterns on sweaters showing simple moss stitching and ribbing reflecting the tiny fields and potato gardens. For the 2011 season, the company revived a hundred-year-old sweater called the 'Máirtín Beag' after a local fisherman who used to wear it. This twinning of older craft with modern design, adapted for contemporary needs, creates something familiar, yet totally new.

Authenticity and Place

/ / We don't just sell knitwear, we sell design and place. In the fashion world, the talk nowadays is about quality, heritage and tradition.

Tarlach de Blacam, 2011[5] */ /*

So how does a company like Inis Meáin selling expensive products 15 miles off the west coast of Ireland survive when practically all Irish clothing companies have either gone to the wall or moved overseas? The secret is style and quality alongside a can-do, self-sufficient attitude and inspiration provided by the hand-craft traditions of Inis Meáin. The company's customers sense the influence of the elements and landscape that so define this island, manifest in intricate, elegant knits.

One reason for so much international interest in Inis Meáin's products is that people realise that while the company uses machinery to enhance production, it always remains faithful to its roots and heritage and the tradition of hand knitting. To discerning buyers, beautiful quality clothing which embodies the unique story and history of a distinctive place is very important. More and more people are interested in finding out where and how a garment was made. Such aspects are becoming more valuable than over-hyped brands.

The emotional and experiential connection between the potential customer and the authenticity of island life is crucial. Inis Meáin creates this sense of connection by showing stunning black and white photographs of the island and islanders to wholesale buyers as a key part of its sales pitch. Clearly, Inis Meáin is selling more than clothes. The stone walls, tiny gardens, fishing boats or currachs and, of course, the clothes and knitting are actually selling an idea, a place where survival depends on dexterity and skill, a place that has bred a fierce independence which in turn inspires an ascetic way of life and a sense of quality.

Yet, in spite of all this, Inis Meáin maintains a practical, grounded approach to business. It handlooms its products on state-of-the-art, Japanese-designed equipment and imports its yarns from a variety of sources, from local providers to those located in the rest of Ireland, Italy and South America.

Tarlach spends three months every year travelling with fellow director Seán Mac Réamoinn to the fashion capitals of the world, showcasing the latest collection of luxurious knitwear at high-profile events like Pitti Uomo, the bi-annual menswear tradeshow in Firenze, and the Bread & Butter tradeshow in Berlin. The company also collaborates with top Italian fashion brand Luciano Barbera, sharing a beautiful showroom on prestigious Fifth Avenue in New York. Levi's creative team even made a visit to the island in 2011 to work on a collaboration between Inis Meáin and Levi's Vintage.

Inis Meáin employs a full-time staff of fifteen people. The company is a multicultural hub where Irish is spoken alongside Italian, German and French. Tarlach feels passionate about the Irish language, a major element in the company's success story.

// It's crazy – I get emails from people in Germany and Japan, and their Irish spelling is a lot better than some Irish people's ... It's a reflection of what has been done to the country – I get down about all the things we are losing, the demise of Irish is a microcosm of that.

Tarlach de Blacam, 2011[6] **//**

Inis Meáin Restaurant & Suites

The clothing company is not the only de Blacam enterprise on Inis Meáin selling 'place'. Tarlach and Áine's son Ruairí and his wife, Marie-Thérèse ('hottest, hippest couple in Irish food' gushed the 2009 *Bridgestone Irish Food Guide[7]*), have created a successful and innovative seasonal business, Inis Meáin Restaurant & Suites. Both the restaurant and five-suite hotel, which offers guests books in lieu of televisions and bicycles in place of van shuttles, are frequent award winners. With an understated building that blends seamlessly into the landscape and a dining room with panoramic views of the island and ocean, they have created what critics call 'Ireland's ultimate destination restaurant' and 'the very best of new Ireland in a part of the country that still feels pleasantly unspoiled.'[8]

The main ingredients used in the restaurant are sourced on the island or in the surrounding seas. Home-grown pork comes from a traditional breed of saddleback pigs, while potatoes and vegetables are grown in small fields sheltered by stone walls. The only fertiliser is seaweed from the shore. Lobster and crab are caught by local fishermen, and scallops come from the Inis Meáin bank less than a mile offshore. The de Blacams have successfully utilised local resources of food, landscape and sense of place, together with their passion and skills, to create a special dining and recreation experience. They have reached qualities of value and service comparable to the best restaurants and guest houses in the world, yet the experiences remain understated but classy. Theirs is a business of authenticity and integrity, whole and uncompromising, loaded with character.

Integrity and character are also seen in the water-harvesting system for the hotel which captures rainwater, and in the bilingual menus. All in all, it is an impressive example of a successful business creating sustainable value rooted in the heritage of a truly distinctive place. In other words, this is an enterprise that successfully balances financial, human and environmental goals, lives its values, acts with integrity and possesses a deep sense of responsibility to the past, present and future.

>❝ What we do looks easy because we make it look easy. But simple is very difficult since everything has to be thought through long and hard. The easier it looks the better we are doing it.
>
> *Ruairí de Blacam, 2011*[9] ❞

Ruairí describes his philosophy in powerful terms, central to which is promising less but giving more so guests' expectations are exceeded. He compares running a restaurant to the stage, a set where you're always on show: 'When the curtain comes up, we the actors are there to help visitors experience Inis Meáin.'[10]

It's a strategy that's working. Nicholas Lander, *Financial Times* food writer and a famous restaurateur, selected it as one of his dozen best restaurants of 2011.[11] Lander's most exceptional memories of the year resonated from an overnight stay on the island and taking a walk past the island's characteristic tiny, stone-walled fields, noting the venture's deep roots in Europe's most western extremity:

// [N]one of this had really prepared me for the sense of place that I felt throughout dinner, triggered initially by a bowl of steamed periwinkles gathered from the shore. Looking up at the far wall I spotted a blown-up black-and-white photograph from 80 years ago of a local fisherman in his windproof sweater, cleaning the periwinkles he had just caught ...

Nicholas Lander, 2011[12] **//**

Conclusion

Both Inis Meáin ventures described above exhibit characteristics which are necessary for the creation and sustenance of successful, globally-competitive, locally-anchored Irish enterprises. True to their roots and heritage, the de Blacams' philosophy is unapologetically Irish yet thoroughly international and cosmopolitan; their enterprises build on Ireland's culture and traditions, yet are not imprisoned by them. They employ heritage and culture in novel, creative and high-quality ways to create value. The de Blacams accomplish this in a place considered by the EU as peripheral and by most as disadvantaged. Most remarkable of all is that they do this in a location which to many represents the very heart and soul of 'old Ireland', capturing in their products the independence, resourcefulness and skills of the islanders among whom they live. It is precisely such rootedness and creative redevelopment of Ireland's culture, heritage and traditions that forms the premise of our argument. Using the Inis Meáin enterprises to introduce this ethic, we discuss in the following chapter how Ireland can best compete internationally by fostering sustainable enterprises based on a locally-rooted identity and adapting their offerings to the modern experience economy.

2

A New Vision of Irish Enterprise

Luigh ar do chranna fortil
I gcoinne mallmhuir is dithrá,
Coigil aithinne d'Aislinge
Scaradh léi is éag duit.

(Lean on your own stout oars
Against neap-tide and ebb,
Keep alight the coal of your vision
To part with that is death.)
Máirtín Ó Direáin, Irish language poet, 1984[1]

Where is the Vision?

This book looks at enterprises that are distinctively Irish, compete fiercely in international markets, sell to the most sophisticated and demanding consumers, and battle world-class rivals. They link past and present, creating products of value for the twenty-first century *experience economy*. Consummately modern, these enterprises harvest the best of the old, combining it with the best of the new.

Such ventures, many unheralded, successfully tap into a rich trove of vision and capability, exemplars of a path intrinsically and authentically Irish. Visionary organisations like the Inis Meáin enterprises profiled in Chapter 1 provide a glimpse into what might be possible, pointing us towards a strand of national development that was given short shrift during the Celtic Tiger years of blessed memory. A balanced and fair economy must include robust indigenous enterprises in addition to multinational giants. These exemplary organisations promise an economy that is in service to a society, exploiting an Irish edge, not only for narrow economic benefit, but for benefits that redound broadly to their community, nation and natural environment.

These organisations come in all sizes, from small farm ventures like Folláin and Country Choice that compete in fresh natural foods and trade on Ireland's significant natural advantages, to large multinationals like the Kerry Group, which is making its huge investment in a Kildare-based global technology and innovation centre central to its global ambitions. They compete in economic sectors as varied as tourism, food ingredients, cultural products, construction materials, traditional crafts and modern digital communications. They exhibit a variety of organisational forms: partnerships and co-operatives, public bodies, profit and non-profit organisations, and privately-held small, as well as huge multinational, companies. Despite these differences, they have one thing in common: they produce products of integrity, grounded in Irish resources or denoted with an Irish brand that simply cannot be duplicated elsewhere – that is, they possess an Irish edge. Yet, in Ireland's rush to embrace still more multinational investment, they are often overlooked or discounted – dismissed with the comment that they are not 'scalable'. Such myopia is unfortunate, for as we show in this book it is precisely these enterprises that offer enormous potential for sustainable economic development.

To clarify this potential, a metaphor is in order. The Hill of Uisneach in County Westmeath, where the four ancient provinces converged at Ireland's centre, was the home of the goddess Ériu, from whom Éire drew its name. In the context of this discussion on Ireland's economic future, Uisneach has deeper significance: it represents a fifth province, a province of the mind, a 'secret centre' where Ireland's essential character, capabilities and sense of place are rooted and where a new Ireland might be envisioned. As philosopher, writer and abbot of Glenstal Abbey Mark Patrick Hederman wrote: 'Uisneach, the secret centre, was the place where all oppositions were resolved ... such a place would require that each person discover it for himself within himself ... It is a place which is beyond or behind the reach of our normal scientific consciousness.'[2] To us, Uisneach is a place of creativity, integrity and self-exploration, where logic and soul, science and art, are in balance. This is why it represents a vision of the new Ireland imagined or hoped for in this book. At its core it is more than a physical or political space; it is a place where the conscious and unconscious are in perfect harmony to ensure Irish people a sustainable, balanced and high quality of life.

In these trying economic times Ireland must reconnect with this province of imagination to see its way forward. A province of imagination rather than geography is a place of possibility and creativity, where opposites come together, clash, get sorted and made whole. In other words, it provides an integrated vision. There is a dearth of such a spirit in contemporary Ireland, which has only a superficial sense of its place in the world and, at best, only a makeshift vision of its future.

What is the zeitgeist of Ireland today? Public policy is staunchly focused on bringing Ireland back to the heady days of the so-called Celtic Tiger, when international delegations made the pilgrimage to see at first hand the Irish miracle and learn the secrets of Ireland's erstwhile success. But this is precisely the *wrong* approach. What is sorely needed instead is a radical new look at Irish development: a vision that *integrates* enterprise, culture and society.

A Third Way

❝ The past is never dead. It's not even past.
William Faulkner, American writer and Nobel laureate, 1951[3] **❞**

First, a caveat: this is not a book about a return to the 'old days and old ways' of an imaginary, romantic 'Celtic Twilight'. Nor do we argue for only one strand of economic policy, advocating a return to *ourselves* or notions of frugal self-sufficiency. Far from it! Yet, an obsession with foreign direct investment to drive development and recovery from the Celtic Tiger's implosion is dangerous and short-sighted. It is equally important to foster indigenous, world-class enterprises.

It is well documented that indigenous firms overall employ significantly more than foreign multinationals, with earnings that tend to be spent at home. These are *not* petty players. For example, the Irish Crafts Council estimates that some 5,770 people are employed in craft enterprises in Ireland with domestic sales of €373 million and exports of €125 million,[4] while for every €1 spent by the Heritage Council, the Irish tourism industry receives €4.40 through increased tourism revenues.[5] One of Ireland's own multinationals, the Kerry Group, employs five thousand people in Ireland and twenty-four thousand globally in one hundred and fifty manufacturing facilities spread over twenty-five countries.

We believe *balanced* development depends neither entirely on the whims of multinationals nor on the exclusive efforts of indigenous enterprise. It is essential to draw proportionate contributions from both. But we must not ignore a crucial third strand: enterprises that either create products and services with a distinctively Irish imprint or make effective use of Ireland's distinctive resources. This book tells *their* stories.

Inspired by culture, these enterprises represent an essential element of a well-functioning and balanced economic system. They are not the only element, and there is plenty of room for multinational investment. Indeed, multinational firms will be more entranced with the possibilities suggested by innovative local firms driven by inimitable resources. Often, foreign firms wish to be seen as local, like Lidl and McDonald's that proudly announce how many of their products are sourced in Ireland. No doubt others will seek to emplace themselves into a creative Irish milieu. But for this to happen, a critical mass of authentic place-based enterprises is necessary.

These enterprises tap into deep sources of competitive advantage, rooted in culture, tradition, identity and sense of place; they create value that is authentic, sustainable and full of character. So, while Ireland needs a mix of multinational corporations and world-class indigenous firms, our focus will largely be on this third strand, on indigenous private, public and community enterprises that utilise Ireland's unique resources in innovative ways and create products and services that are uniquely if not quintessentially 'Irish'. These firms build up, and build upon, their Irish edge.

Recent policy developments, however, inspire little confidence. Legislation now stipulates that employees of multinationals transferring to Ireland for up to five years qualify for generous tax relief, while companies claiming tax relief on research and development (R&D) spending are able to transfer benefits to specified 'key employees'. But do such perks create vast numbers of jobs? This is certainly open to question, but these actions clearly suggest that jobs created by foreign companies are valued more than those created by Irish firms. This is symptomatic of an unhealthy fixation on foreign investment to the detriment of indigenous industry, the contributions of which are too often taken for granted.

Local retailers, in particular, are under considerable stress, with over thirty thousand jobs lost over the past five years. With planning approval for larger facilities and the ability to sell certain items below cost, big-box foreign retailers are finding Ireland increasingly attractive. But hypermarkets kill footfall in urban centres and often rip the heart out of main streets in towns and villages, leading to the loss of Ireland's unique heritage of shop-front lettering and painted signage.[6] No doubt there will be many more closures as distinctive places, which are great draws for tourists, are consigned to the dustbin of history. Surely such places not only tug at emotional heartstrings but also have considerable economic value?

Other countries have far more effective planning and retail entry restrictions; they know how to protect their uniqueness. They value and build on their inheritance without being trapped by the past. France applies strict store size limits, while in Italy, independent, family-run retailers remain an essential element in every-day urban life. It is hard for chain stores to open in these countries, and massive out-of-town shopping malls are rare. These countries realise where their strengths lie.

Is it any wonder that Ireland's share of the world tourist market has plummeted, despite spending more money per capita on tourism marketing than any other European country? Its marketing spend per arrival is almost eight times that of France and nineteen times that of Italy.[7] Ireland gets only 0.5 repeat visits for every first-time visitor, compared to 4.5 for Spain and 2.0 for Scotland.[8] Why is this? Clearly, something is out of joint.

❚❚ If we think that tourists – particularly the diaspora – who support over a quarter of a million jobs will pay Irish prices so that they can spend their holidays watching English soccer in our pubs and hotel lounges, we've got another think [*sic*] coming.

Marc Coleman, economist and columnist, 2010[9] **❚❚**

One reason for the low level of return visitors is that Ireland is simply losing its sense of distinctiveness. Talk about 'Irishness' is considered by many to be alright in the context of

Fáilte Ireland's marketing of 'The Gathering' or the Island of Saints and Scholars, but of dubious value in the 'real world'. In fact, to talk of Irishness exposes the speaker to immediate dismissal as a woolly-minded romantic with his head in a Celtic mist. No wonder Marc Coleman warns that Ireland is in danger of drifting into a mid-Atlantic no man's land. If the country is to be a serious competitor in the global cultural tourism market, it must cultivate, not bulldoze, its own distinctiveness. It should not be jettisoning its past, but building upon it; not moving back *to it*, but forward *with it*.

As a Fáilte Ireland economist argues, 'We need a clear sense of what it means to be Irish and what makes us different, otherwise it is "me too" time.'[10] Mere imitation does not make for repeat business in the tourist trade. What will do it is distinctiveness, sense of place and character: a culture grounded in authenticity rather than caricature created to attract tourists and foreign investors, what one commentator dubbed 'biscuit tin folklore'.[11] Tourists are not dumb; they sense what is real and what is not. The enterprises profiled in this book, like the Inis Meáin ventures discussed in Chapter 1, recognise this and build products and experiences of character, quality and integrity.

❝ It is unacceptable that we still do not have a sense of who we are and what we stand for.
Joe Carr, partner at international consultants Mazars, 2009[12] *❞*

An Economic Aisling

Contrary to what outsiders often assume, fear of the past is very prevalent in Ireland, particularly in business circles. This is not surprising; after all, the prevailing ideology of globalisation treats national culture as an outmoded concept. Those who dare speak of national identity are often accused of trying to drag Ireland back to a de Valerian Gaelic age complete with social suffocation and economic stagnation.

This is easy enough to understand, given Ireland's economic experience through most of the twentieth century. It is no wonder that the country has adopted a 'one-size-fits-all' model of development, betting on foreign direct investment rather than indigenous capabilities to restart its troubled economy. After all, didn't such a strategy work before?

Ireland can do better, but it needs a more balanced, distinctive approach. There are many paths to prosperity, and Ireland has a unique journey to take. For development to be sustainable, and for a successful society to endure, Ireland must choose an economic path that builds upon its culture, is consistent with its aspirations, respects its traditions, and leverages its sense of place. Only this will foster truly sustainable development.

Character and Integrity

❮❮ The word integrity comes from the same Latin root as 'integer' and historically has been understood to carry much the same sense; the sense of wholeness: a person of integrity, like a whole number, is a whole person, a person somehow undivided.
Stephen L. Carter, Professor of Law at Yale University, 1996[13] *❯❯*

Admittedly, notions like integrity, character and authenticity are slippery; they rarely appear in the Irish business lexicon. Indeed, if used at all (in advertising, marketing or 'reputation management') they are likely to be abused, compromised or distorted in ways that drain them of utility. However, we understand them differently and illustrate this with Irish enterprises, such as Cnoc Suain (tourism) and Molloy & Sons (craft), that embrace integrity and authenticity as essential elements of their global advantage.

Authenticity reflects the quality seen, felt and sensed in a product. But how can integrity, character and authenticity be achieved? The answer: from within rather than without.

While authenticity is often seen as fixed, it is better viewed as a set of contradictions: static but changing, conservative but adaptable, original but modern. While the inauthentic is broken, the authentic is whole. An intangible ethic of excellence is at the core of quality, wholeness and integrity, a sense of duty or commitment to oneself and others past, present and future. Authenticity means being willing to do the right thing even at personal cost. This requires people to have meaning in their lives, a wholeness derived from internal standards of self-respect, self-reliance and self-sacrifice.

The development of character founded on dignity, self-confidence, self-respect and self-reliance is surely as important as a low corporate tax rate. To suggest that business people must choose between compliance with 'progressive' international imperatives or faithfulness to 'backward' indigenous values offers a false and cynical dichotomy. Instead, to be global, cosmopolitan and economically successful, there should be a renewed emphasis on the development of indigenous Irish firms that utilise Ireland's distinctive cultural identity and heritage. This is not romanticism; it is a practical approach to developing high-calibre indigenous enterprises that can hold their own internationally.

Countries with character and integrity accept their moral duties to future generations while also learning from the past. Becoming a successful player in a globalising world does not require that Ireland relinquish its immensely rich culture and traditions and an identity built over centuries. However, as the *Irish Times* notes, Ireland lacks 'an overarching political vision that links a knowledge and appreciation of the past with the provision of jobs, local development and a better future.'[14]

" There will be no recovery worth its name without the spiritual, moral and cultural dimensions which renew Ireland's self-understanding and confidence.

Irish Times, *2011*[15]

Yet, Ireland does possess a distinctive edge. Culture, identity and sense of place can foster creativity and innovation as surely as high-tech research laboratories. Science and technology, of course, are critical and necessary, but Ireland must also realise the potential of resources that are truly unique and inimitable, and offer something different on the world stage. Such resources *support* learning in science and technology, and offer indigenous firms – particularly in sectors like tourism, food and drink, entertainment, media and craft, and the budding 'green' or environmentally-sustainable business sector – opportunities to develop and market products that are distinctive, authentic and full of character. These products are ineffably Irish, locally-rooted but world-class, and sold into a global marketplace that values quality, design, distinctiveness and authenticity. Indigenous enterprises selling such products are not unknown in this country, but due to government priorities they are rarely given the support or space they need to grow to full potential. This is not so for countries like France and Italy which use both their authenticity and distinctiveness to promote tourism and indigenous enterprises.

The Experience Economy

It is worth examining the idea of the experience economy in more detail since it is fundamental to a different way of thinking about Irish development. In the experience economy, value rises as meaning deepens, moving from scientific knowledge founded on information and rationality to *wisdom* which is informed by purpose, ethics, memory and vision.[16] While information is mechanistic and abundant, wisdom is holistic and scarce, and promoted by the arts.

In the twenty-first-century digital economy, consumers want valuable experiences more than tangible products per se. Indeed, the search for meaning is a core economic driver as we undergo a paradigm shift – from a techno-economic age founded on physical goods to a sustainable age of intangible experiences. Emotional values are now the driver and rational values the passengers.[17] In a quest for self-realisation, individuals want to spend time and money on compelling experiences, not commoditised goods and services. Making sense matters far more than making mere stuff! Empathy and emotion also matter as people look for sensation-filled experiences that engage them in memorable ways.

Such experiences are inherently personal and exist only in the minds of people when they are fully engaged – emotionally, physically, intellectually and spiritually. As with any stage production, no two people have the same experience; this derives from the relationship between the performance and people's responses to it. The emerging economic era is one where patterns, context and the symbolic are crucial. More than ever, strong personal feelings and the ability to foster relationships are paramount; emphasis is on intangibility, trust, aesthetics, judgement and self-knowledge.

As the significance of the material diminishes and capacities of the mind become a crucial competitive factor, meaning, experience and identity will become key to competitiveness and innovation. Imagination, the most valuable resource of all, is driven by emotions and feelings, the heart rather than the rational mind, and mostly nurtured through the arts. It is a resource founded on inspiration, empathy, tradition and trust, rooted in the social and economic fabric of relationships.

The Internet has amplified this trend, ensuring that intangibles are mobile and tradable. Storytelling, metaphor, conversation, reflection, development of character and an ethic of quality are essential components of what best-selling author Daniel Pink calls a 'whole new mind'.[18]

// Meaning is the new money.

Daniel Pink, American author, 2003[19] **//**

Everyday examples of products where the experience is a major component of value include French fashion, Swiss watches or Italian cuisine. The information age does not only mean information mediated by computers but also includes the increasing significance of the symbolic level of products themselves. Such information is in the sense of experiences and meanings mediated by physical products. So it is no surprise that IT companies often spend more on promoting symbols than on technical development per se. Buying a mobile phone, for instance, is very much about buying a certain experience, meaning or identity. In its heyday, Nokia's success in capturing a huge chunk of the mobile phone market was based on understanding this, marrying Finnish competence in design with breakthrough technology.[20] Progressive businesses recognise that the best way to differentiate their products and services is to infuse them with emotion and artistry. The late Steve Jobs of Apple was brilliant at doing this. He consistently embedded passion and poetry in Apple's products, helping to create engaging experiences for buyers. In his era the iPad or iPhone were status symbols, so the decision to buy was more about emotions such as pride and loyalty than about performance or price.

// Steve was always, if not an artist, then someone who was charmed by style. He had this dream of something beautiful ... his legacy will be the blending of technology and poetry ... he shifted the industry and changed our lives through this amalgamation of culture and technology.

New York Times, 2011[21] **//**

Orthodox enterprises remain wedded to rationality and control rather than emotions, empathy and relationships. They see intangible resources, especially the knowledge and skills of people, as a means to leverage value out of tangible resources. In contrast, the modern network enterprise, deeply interconnected both internally and externally, uses tangibles to leverage value out of intangibles. Indeed, corporate value is increasingly tied up in intangibles like culture, relationships and brands. For many enterprises, intangibles represent a great untapped source of competitive advantage. Central to this is a heightened sensitivity to cultural uniqueness; it is critical. Not surprising then that Paul Rellis, managing director of Microsoft Ireland, suggests that an ability to work cross-culturally is as important as technical skills. He believes that Ireland already possesses the ingredients to become a leading digital economy:

// [Ireland] has the technical knowledge, know-how, the literary, artistic, and musical skill, and the cultural agility to successfully interact with people across the globe.
Paul Rellis, 2008[22] **//**

We agree, yet it is unlikely that the Irish will value cultural uniqueness abroad unless they also value it at home. This is the real challenge and a key message of this book.

Reviving the Revival Spirit

Ireland is badly in need of the driving vision that characterised the Irish Revival of the three decades before Independence. The Revival was an exhilarating time – a mix of creativity, cultural renaissance, idealism and self-help – that encompassed a range of initiatives in commerce, agriculture, theatre, literature, sport and language. At its core was the idea that cultural self-belief was fundamental to development.[23] Organisations like the Gaelic Athletic Association (GAA), Gaelic League, Co-operative Movement, the Irish Literary (later Abbey) Theatre and various scientific societies were cut from a similar cloth. Common to all was a sense of place and pride, stretching from local to national level.

These organisations attracted an eclectic array of individuals, with a sense of identity and national purpose binding them in a common enterprise. Among the characteristics that they shared, the foremost was self-reliance: the notion that the responsibility for development resided in Irish, not foreign, hands. A shared identity and sense of place were prerequisites to the development of self-reliance and necessary for innovativeness. Horace Plunkett espoused a commercial ethos, moral courage and thrift as core elements in his vision of the Co-operative Movement. In founding the Irish Agricultural Organisation Society (IAOS) in 1894, Plunkett saw the co-operative form of organisation as an ideal way to help turn the Irish character towards commercial habits of quality and self-reliance. Yet, years later, comparing lack of progress in Ireland to Denmark, he accepted that the ground would have been better prepared for co-operation if a mission-driven education movement had been set up in advance of his co-operative movement.[24] Even so, throughout Irish industry, a spirit of interdependence and innovativeness came alive.

There are exemplary contemporary organisations tracing their lineage directly to this Revival spirit. The GAA, arguably the world's most successful amateur sports organisation and Ireland's most impressive socio-cultural movement, is one.

Gaelic Athletic Association (GAA)

The GAA is hugely popular. It has successfully triumphed in Ireland over stiff competition from other sports like soccer and rugby with huge international followings. It is home-grown, deeply meaningful and unabashedly Irish. During the Revival, the GAA fostered rootedness by creating local sporting contests that captured the emotions, especially of young people, and added colour and excitement to an often dull rural social life. It promoted a robust Irish identity through teamwork and co-operation, deeply rooted in a hierarchy of local communities and conducive to cultural self-knowledge and self-reliance. The organisation's founding father, Michael Cusack, saw national morale, a sense of community and a spirit of self-sufficiency as central to economic renewal. Today, even with the GAA's relative affluence, this attachment to place and grassroots democracy persists. It remains a locally-rooted, community-centred organisation, dependent on volunteerism and based on democratic principles of governance. In a globalised world, the GAA's continued success can be attributed to a passionate commitment to the local. Sociologist Tom Inglis maintains that when visitors come to Ireland and see the county colours paraded and hear the banter of the locals they realise that it is the GAA – not language, music or religion – which makes the Irish different.[25]

The GAA is a unique institution, a fact not appreciated by many Irish people. Yet, outsiders are often filled with admiration and awe at its success in drawing passionate support while retaining its amateur ethos, as was Zack O'Malley Greenburg, a writer for US business magazine *Forbes*, after attending his first Gaelic football match:

❝ For someone such as myself, who makes a living by studying and chronicling the monetization of success and fame, it's hard not to find fascination in a cursory examination of Gaelic football. In many ways, the state of the sport resembles the early days of American athletics, when most players were paid so little they had to work in the offseason … But perhaps a fundamental miscalculation lies in the assumption that all cultures value fame as America does – something that could and should be monetized. Though it may seem naïve to assume, perhaps glory really is worth more to some than to others …

Zack O'Malley Greenburg, 2011[26] **❞**

Croke Park

The GAA knows what it is and where it is. With deep roots in Irish communities throughout the country (and abroad), it possesses the ability to continually reinvent itself to ensure its long-term vitality and relevance. The story of Croke Park, the organisation's home in Dublin since matches were first played there in 1896, is a remarkable example of this ability. The stadium's troubled history, such as the shooting dead by British forces of thirteen civilians, including player Michael Hogan, on 'Bloody Sunday' in 1920, remains firmly lodged in the nation's psyche, reinforcing a sense of connection with the place. This sense surely plays a huge role in encouraging people to attend non-sporting events there, such as major conferences and exhibitions.

The third largest stadium in Europe, Croke Park attracts crowds of eighty-two thousand or more to major hurling and football fixtures. All-Ireland day, in particular, is a uniquely Irish event. However, as probably the most important cultural location in Ireland, Croke Park is no ordinary sports stadium. Its 'hallowed ground' is truly the spirit of a nation; no other ground offers so rich a heritage or possesses such cultural significance. For many Irish people, it is simply the most important single place in Ireland, their own contemporary Hill of Tara. Such a place has an inspiring effect on players who see playing there as the ultimate sporting privilege, often the pinnacle of their careers. As legendary commentator Micheál Ó Muircheartaigh says:

❝ Croke Park signifies the Mecca of national community to most Irish people ... In explaining the significance of Croke Park to other people, I ask them to envisage all they hold dear as part of their own culture and then contemplate Croke Park as the epitome of Irish sporting culture and pride.

Micheál Ó Muircheartaigh, retired RTÉ sports commentator, 2007[27] **❞**

It's no surprise that the Queen of England made a particular statement by visiting 'Croker' on her historic Irish visit in May 2011. Until 2007, only GAA games were allowed to be played in Croke Park, but that year it opened its doors to soccer and rugby while their own ground was being redeveloped. The standing to attention of the Irish and English rugby teams for the playing of 'God Save the Queen' was a leap forward in the political relationship between the countries and a measure of newfound Irish self-confidence. It does make us wonder what that stalwart nationalist, Archbishop of Cashel Dr Thomas Croke, in whose memory the stadium is named, would make of it all:

// Indeed if we continue travelling for the next score years in the same direction that we have been going in for some time past, condemning the sports that were practised by our forefathers, effacing our national features as though we were ashamed of them, and putting on, with England's stuffs and broadcloths, her masher habits and such other effeminate follies as she may recommend, we had better at once, and publicly, abjure our nationality, clap hands for joy at the sight of the Union Jack, and place 'England's bloody red' exultantly above the green.
Dr Thomas Croke, Former Archbishop of Cashel, 1884[28] **//**

The GAA's activities and its iconic Croke Park continue to inspire. In the early 1990s the GAA came up with a visionary plan to redevelop Croke Park into a modern stadium. Today, Croke Park combines one of Europe's finest stadiums, and Dublin's largest meeting venue, with luxury accommodation, a conference centre, GAA museum, and more. In 2010 it gained certification as the world's first stadium to receive the prestigious British Standard award for sustainable event management (BS 8901), an example for other stadiums to emulate.

The Second Revival

A more recent example of Ireland's revival spirit is the resurgent self-confidence of the late fifties and sixties that found expression in what Irish brand expert John Fanning calls the Second Revival.[29] This loose movement saw many noteworthy attempts at cultural revival, often against severe odds, led by remarkable individuals. Those in its vanguard possessed a highly sophisticated sense of tradition and did not ignore the global but saw it through the lens of Irish culture and heritage. A critical element in the new revival was an active opening out to the rest of the world following three decades of withdrawal.

This opening out was exemplified by the lives of three men whose careers and personal lives crossed during that time, namely T.K. Whitaker, Seán Ó Riada and Thomas Kinsella. Secretary of the Department of Finance T.K. Whitaker played a pivotal role in the impetus to economic growth in the 1960s. Composer and musician Seán Ó Riada's slim but significant musical output transformed Irish traditional music, provided the country with much-needed self-confidence and inspired numerous musical groups to export Irish music to every corner of the world. The outstanding artistic figure of post-war Ireland, Ó Riada had a highly developed regard for tradition, fusing native and international music forms.[30] Poet and publisher Thomas Kinsella ploughed a lonelier furrow, but his translations of ancient Irish literature performed a similar, albeit lower key, role to Ó Riada's. All three men shared two key characteristics: an intense curiosity about developments in their chosen fields around the world and a thorough knowledge of, and passionate attachment to, Irish literature, language, history and culture. As Seán Ó Riada said in his 1962 broadcast for the RTÉ radio series *Our Musical Heritage*:

❝ What of our traditions do, in fact, survive? Our way of life, and our customs, are being thrown out in favour of

an alien materialism. Our hospitality, at least in the urban areas, is long forgotten, a joke. Our language is made the excuse for cynical hypocrisy. Our literature is giving over mainly to aping foreign models. Our nation, that was bought with blood, is being sold, spiritually as well as physically, before our own eyes, by our own people. This is a great evil, a great madness. The strongest surviving tradition is our music. We must not let it go. And it is up to ourselves to keep it. We have too long been looking for help from elsewhere.

Seán Ó Riada, 1982[31] *"*

Fr James McDyer

The spirit of the Second Revival is illuminated by Fr James McDyer's radical activities during the 1960s in Gleann Cholm Cille, County Donegal. McDyer focused on this place's infrastructural defects, particularly roads, social amenities and water schemes. With local support, he built a folk museum, holiday village, hotel and vegetable-processing factory, which was supplied by local landowners who co-operated to grow vegetables. The factory was a radical development and seen by activists in other marginal communities as the best way to advance the cause of self-help.

Gael Linn

The organisation Gael Linn, very active in the 1960s, also illuminates the spirit of the Second Revival. Gael Linn was one of the most influential and dynamic organisations with a spirit of self-reliance underpinning its work. It fostered a range of ventures through the Irish language in film-making, musical recordings, general cultural activities and socio-economic projects such as fish and vegetable processing, seaweed processing, bee-keeping and holiday properties. In the early 1960s, Gael Linn even applied for the licence to run Ireland's first television channel, but the government decided to establish Teilifís Éireann instead.

Kilkenny Design Workshops

The Second Revival led to the establishment of innovative organisations such as Córas Tráchtala (Irish Export Board), IDA Ireland and the Kilkenny Design Workshops (KDWs), to mention just a few in the state-supported sector. Especially valuable insights into the spirit of the Second Revival may be gleaned from the history of the KDWs. As state-sponsored design consultancies aimed at improving the design of Irish products and increasing exports, they were founded in 1963 by Córas Tráchtála. Their creator and first chief executive was a former general manager of Córas Tráchtála, William H. Walsh. Walsh was an implacable foe of that 'sure it'll do' strain of Irishness.[32] It was his idea to tap leading Scandinavian industrial designers for advice on improving the standards of Irish design. In the foreword to the resultant report, Walsh summed up nicely the idea that while good design is an undeniable necessity for the growth of exports, standards cannot be raised for exports only:

> The factors which determine the quality, good or bad, of the designs we produce are deeply rooted in our homes, our schools, our shops, our historical traditions, our whole way of living.
>
> *William H. Walsh, 1961*[33]

The report cautioned against shallow utilisation of old or foreign models, warning that these never lead to the creation of anything of value; instead, the report urged the country to market products that were out of the ordinary, with a distinct Irish quality or characteristics. It found that the best designed products in Ireland came from craft industries that successfully interpreted tradition, such as Donegal tweeds and hand-knitted sweaters. By harnessing the ideas of leading international designers, yet inspired by all that was good in the native tradition, the KDWs – until their demise in 1988 – had an impact on Irish industrial design, aesthetics and environmental sensitivity out of proportion to the resources devoted to them.

The Third Revival

Greater awareness and the practical application of Ireland's cultural heritage must be a vital component of any Third Revival. Combining traditional knowledge and craft skills with modern design would re-energise Ireland's cultural heritage and provide the impetus for a much-needed boost to the indigenous business sector, thereby reducing Ireland's dependence on foreign direct investment. John Fanning maintains that it's a sure sign of self-confidence when local products and brands are successful, but signals defeatism when people think that good things only come from abroad.[34] A greater awareness of cultural heritage translates into confidence in the goods and services produced in the society.

Thus, the Irish will achieve their full potential when they absorb the best of what the rest of the world has to offer but filter this knowledge and experience through a deep understanding of their own history and cultural traditions. For Ireland to flourish, Fanning holds, it is necessary for Irish people to possess an intense appreciation and understanding of who they are and where they come from, combined with an insatiable curiosity about what is happening in the rest of the world. Like us, Fanning maintains that if a Third Revival is to happen, it will be intimately connected to culture, tradition and place, just like the first and second Revivals.

The potency of how this ideology can be achieved is best illustrated by Nordic countries which have long recognised that cultural repossession and rejuvenation are necessary to develop a spirit of national self-reliance and self-confidence. This manifests itself in not being bound by short-term economic thinking, narrow perspectives on the arts or utilitarian approaches to education. Unlike Ireland, Finland and Denmark – also small countries – have developed deep indigenous industrial bases. Witness also the creative success of all Nordic countries in going from cultural backwaters to powerhouses, home to blockbuster international hits like Danish television show *The Killing* and Finnish video game *Angry Birds*. Noma in Copenhagen is now rated among the world's top restaurants. Its head chef collects local products such as mushrooms, cloudberries and seaweed from beaches and hedgerows, saying his guests should 'experience something that can only happen in this particular part of the world and in this particular city.'[35]

Who am I, What am I, Where am I?

The backstory of any product, where it comes from, who made it, how it was made and what materials were used, is becoming increasingly important. Take Harris Tweed, the coarse-chequered cloth produced for centuries in the tiny Outer Hebrides island of Harris. It was once the favoured attire of the upper classes and country gentlemen, but over time, with changes in fashion and the advent of softer fabrics, demand for tweed declined, and many producers simply withered away. Enter Nike, the giant sportswear manufacturer, who chose Harris Tweed in 2004 to adorn one of its latest designer trainers, generating a turnaround in the fortunes of this unique industry. Tradition sells; being distinctive, it seems, is half the battle!

// You associate Nike with very hi-tech trainers, and so to have this sort of almost peasantry looking kind of shoe, I think is really interesting.
Harriet Quick, fashion features director at Vogue, 2004[36] **//**

Global enterprises are often embedded in local history, culture and ecology. Look at famed Scandinavian-designed home-furnishings company IKEA. This company's soul, maintains founder Ingvar Kamprad, emerges from the traditional and enduring handmade stone fences characteristic of his birthplace, rural Småland.[37] Solid fences there are built from thousands of individual rocks, each lifted from the rocky soil of the Swedish countryside. Rooted in the soil, built one at a time over the centuries, these stone walls serve as a continual symbol of the company's spirit, described as follows: 'The people are famous for working hard, living on slender means and using their heads to make the best possible use of the limited resources they have. This way of doing things is at the heart of the IKEA approach to keeping prices low.'[38] Surely something similar inspires major Irish multinationals like the Kerry Group, Kingspan or Glen Dimplex?

France and Italy have great reputations for distinctive artisanal industries, captured by the concept of *terroir*, and embodied in characteristic qualities specific to local environments. Such economic activities are complex and rich, culturally and naturally rooted, and simply inimitable. The wines, champagne, beers, cheeses, breads and other food products possess subtle nuances and characteristics attributable to their place of origin.

Likewise, a pronounced regional identity motivated people in West Cork over a decade ago to develop the Fuchsia brand ('West Cork ... a place apart') to capture a clear connection between the place and its products. The fuchsia, long associated with West Cork, was chosen to represent a symbol of quality for food products, such as black pudding, which are 'firmly rooted in the unique traditions and influences of the region.'[39]

Market-driven but mission-centred, enterprises in special places invariably possess a deep values-based orientation, providing a catalyst to build vibrant communities. By nurturing the intrinsic qualities of their own place, such enterprises deliver long-term value to their communities.

They sustain resources, striving to improve the places they call home. Important components of a competitive, world-class indigenous sector, they deliver valuable experiences to discerning global consumers through the integrity, character and authenticity that are hallmarks of their operations.

❝ In a world where almost anything could be made anywhere, identity is everything.
Peter Mandelson, former EU Trade Commissioner, 2007[40] **❞**

Sargadelos

We see this phenomenon of place-based enterprises throughout Europe. Spanish firm Sargadelos, based in Galicia, is one of the most distinctive porcelain design and creation companies in Europe. Its development closely parallels nearly two hundred years of Galician culture. Sargadelos opened its first factory early in the nineteenth century, transforming rich Galician clay into innovative, decorative chinaware. Today, it still uses authentic motifs, forms and colours that are rooted in Galician culture and tradition. It maintains an international reputation alongside a dynamic, place-based ethos. In this sense it is much like the Inis Meáin knitwear company profiled earlier, which holds its own with the world's top fashion houses, with designs inspired by the traditional craft of its small Aran Island community.

Heath Ceramics

Even products manufactured in one of the most expensive locations in the US can successfully compete with cheaper imports when they are high-end, craft-based *and* accompanied by a great story about being made in America. Take, for instance, Heath Ceramics of Sausalito, California. This company was founded by the late Edith Heath in 1948. Heath, a talented ceramicist with a great respect for craft and material, and a mentality moulded by experiences during the Great Depression, was motivated to design and produce long-lasting products, made with integrity in a responsible manner. As the company website puts it: 'simple, good things for good people.'[41]

Heath's iconic name is synonymous with functional and thoughtfully designed tableware and tiles with clean, modernist lines which represent a fresh break from the more fussy designs of the past. Many of Edith's original pieces live in the permanent collections of museums like the prestigious Museum of Modern Art (MOMA) in New York. When Robin Petravic and his wife Catherine took over the business in 2003, Heath's high quality, durable pieces that blur the line between everyday objects and family heirlooms were still being made by craftspeople – many of whom had worked for Heath for decades – in small runs, in a sustainable, labour-intensive manner in the original Sausalito premises, just as they had been since 1948.[42] However, the couple decided that Heath's idiosyncratic way of doing things and the company's geographical roots were strengths, not weaknesses. This was not an orthodox approach, particularly as global competition had forced most American-based artisan potteries to close. The couple discovered that consumers were increasingly interested in home-grown products and their unique stories, and Heath Ceramics was well positioned to supply both.

More and more, authenticity and experience matter to the modern consumer. Dublin-based craftsperson Jennifer Slattery, for instance, bored by the uniformity of modern design, is attracted to flaws and imperfections that exude genuine character. She is inspired by what has gone before, and realising that there *is* a future in the Irish past, designs nostalgic but contemporary textiles. Such an appreciation seems rarely recognised by Irish leaders as they encourage businesses to grasp opportunities in emerging markets like Asia.

// Price is what you pay. Value is what you get.

Warren Buffet, 2008[43] **//**

Creative Places

Inheriting a strong sense of identity helps people reflect on their place in the world so they can better manage uncertainty about the future. It spurs a spirit of self-discovery and an innovative frame of mind, contributing to integrity, civic responsibility, aesthetic sensibility, ecological stewardship, ethical behaviour and resourcefulness. A country's wisdom, values and cultural self-knowledge offer breadth, purpose and confidence. Individuals with meaning in their lives and a sense of continuity between past and present build more trusting and caring communities. Standards become internal, deriving impetus from integrity, tradition, community, empathy and intergenerational solidarity. It's a good reason why private animation and television production company Telegael, the Irish-language state broadcaster TG4, and the predominantly voluntary GAA are all crucial to the development of local communities.

This ethos of integrity emerges through a deep-seated sense of place – a *genius loci*, the soul of a place. Such a sense encompasses a shared experience of history and community, representing a deep emotional attachment to a particular place. It is complicated, holistic and multi-layered, dense with meaning. And it is more than just a romantic idea! Not only does a sense of place help make lives worthwhile, but it provides people and organisations with tangible economic advantages. A sense of place matters: it drives decisions that impact the care and preservation of the natural, built and cultural environments. It also affects those attributes of a living, breathing community that foster innovation, creativity and sustainability. Those with a deep commitment to a place can utilise the implicit knowledge and wisdom embedded there.

❝ Place isn't an abstract concept. On the contrary, it's where all the big things come together – economics and society, the past and the present, the idea of what is distinctive with the idea of a shared space. And one of the things we screwed up so mightily in the boom years was this sense of place. Putting 300 suburban houses on the edge of an old village of 200 houses and leaving the whole thing as a ghost estate, is what happens when a sense of place is lost.

Fintan O'Toole, Irish Times journalist, 2011[44] **"**

We are shaped by our places, and we in turn shape them. Place provides an integrated eco-system where all forms of creativity – artistic and cultural, technological and economic – take root and flourish. Those places that succeed emphasise culture, attracting and keeping creative people through the qualities of a diverse, authentic and unique community. This then attracts enterprise, reversing the traditional direction of development. A good example of a creative place is Dingle (An Daingean), County Kerry. The only access town to Corca Dhuibhne, an iconic, Irish-speaking peninsula with mist-covered mountains at its back, a neat sheltered harbour at its front, hilly streets, brightly coloured houses and cosy pubs with traditional music, it is no surprise this small fishing town, the most westerly in Europe, was cited as the most beautiful place on earth by the *National Geographic Traveler* magazine.[45] No surprise either that its Other Voices festival, a seminal TV series recorded in the town in early December every year, attracts the world's top musical talent. We wonder if they would come to Dublin. Even if they did, as journalist Tony Clayton-Lea put it, people 'wouldn't get within an ass's roar' of them there![46]

In the past, a key strategic imperative of business growth was cost reduction or clustering companies in industrial estates. But, today, a unique innovating network that fosters resourcefulness is more likely to enhance a country, region or city's competitiveness. Examples of how unique places combine with an ethic of sustainability to inspire an innovating network include Le Quartier de la Création in Nantes,

France and Arabianranta Creative Quarter in Helsinki, Finland.[47] Such creative places represent authentic, distinctive and unique milieus, emerging from tradition and rootedness, and founded on identity, empathy, emotions and trust.

Why Culture Counts

As the significance of materialism diminishes in a post-Celtic Tiger Ireland and creative capacities of the mind rise in importance, individual attitudes and a sense of meaning shaped by communities and traditions loom large. A strong cultural identity emerges when questions like 'where do I come from?', 'who are my people?', and 'what are their values?' are asked. Tangling with these questions allows meaning and identity to emerge, leading to a strong sense of place founded on memory, tradition and belonging.

No doubt, sceptics will contend that the concept of an Irish sense of place, if it exists at all, is limited to *gaeilgeoirí* pining for an Ireland of thatched cottages and myth. This is simply not so: a shared sense of place can provide real competitive advantages, especially in an innovation age. Creative people are clustering in places which offer authenticity and uniqueness, attracted by this shared sense of community. For example, Portland, Oregon, with its temperate climate, vibrant arts scene, status as craft-beer capital, liberal political values and reputation as the 'greenest city in America', ranks high by this measure. Even during the recent recession, Portland's local independent restaurants and manufacturers increased sales and opened new outlets.[48] But Ireland of the Celtic Tiger years exhibited only a fractured, tortured and even delusional sense of place, creating a *placeless* view of itself – a state characterised by standardisation and uniformity, lack of emotional attachment and increasing mobility. In becoming one of the most globalised economies in the world, Ireland's sense of its own distinctiveness and authenticity weakened.

At the height of the boom, historian Joe Lee observed that the young professionals riding its crest were 'the first generation of Irish that had never known defeat.'[49] He was right; but that was then. Now, that same generation has ample opportunity to stare defeat in the eye. Ireland's descent into severe recession has changed everything. Even worse, this crisis was largely self-inflicted. As film director Neil Jordan said at the first Global Irish Economic Forum at Farmleigh in 2009, people were let down by banks, politicians, the construction industry and the Church: 'So many institutions have failed the Irish people. The culture industry, they have not failed, they are perhaps the only success story that remains after the last 20 years.'[50]

// Has Brien Friel let us down ... have the Chieftains, Maeve Binchy, Marian Keyes?

Colm Tóibín, Irish novelist and short story writer, 2009[51] **//**

Ireland's culture is a significant and deeply-rooted resource, a unique advantage that could foster a revival no less globally competitive for being authentically Irish. Yet, it is precisely this resource that was taken for granted and damaged by the boom. Many policymakers and business people still treat culture as an asset to be monetised and purveyed to a global market. Such 'Disneyisation' of Irish culture is clearly related to a profound lack of appreciation for its deeper value.

Realising the Smart Economy

By their own admission, the value system which economists promote is narrow, crude and pragmatic, leaving little room for insight, imagination or inspiration.[52] Their models ignore the complexities and mysteries of human behaviour, and assume that people are simple and rational beings, only interested in satisfying individualistic needs. The knowledge people possess is regarded as valuable only in so far as it helps them achieve such selfish desires. Of course, knowledge *is* a fundamental source of inimitable advantage, but the nature of that knowledge is difficult for economists trained in industrial-age thinking to grasp. Consequently, they emphasise rational rather than non-rational elements such as ingenuity, self-assurance, self-respect and self-confidence. But it is the latter that are really distinctive and least susceptible to imitation, since they are rooted in the social fabric of local cultural and social relationships.

A big mistake is to assume innovation springs primarily from the rational mind. New ideas and creative impulses are more likely to begin with emotions or feelings. In other words, innovation is as much about the heart as the head, driven by stories that create a rich visual imagery, an ideal base for creativity. The soul is fed by stories, the mind by logic. Powerful stories which feed the imagination and lead to innovation emerge from meanings and experiences associated with a special place. However, policymakers focus on scientific research based on objectivity, denying the legitimacy of the subjective world of feeling and ignoring Ireland's distinct and valuable resources: a sense of connection and imagination.[53] This is why literature, music, the arts and humanities are marginalised in contemporary Irish society, playing a distant role to science and technology.

While scientific research is important, breakthrough ideas require intelligence of the heart and hand, not just intelligence of the head. Emotions, taste, sensations and feelings, which come from the heart rather than the rational mind, are primary drivers of creativity and innovation. To think creatively we need to weaken conventional thought; to do so, we must embrace and harness ambiguity, ambivalence, counter-intuitive thinking and paradox. These are characteristics with which, let's face it, the Irish have long been acquainted.

The reality borders on the tragic: Irish leaders fail to recognise that the country possesses precisely those distinctive, inimitable and rare resources ideally suited for success in the emerging conceptual era. In the imaginative age, a refusal to accept the conventional is crucial and best nurtured through poetry, literature, drama, music and the arts. Ireland's tradition of narrative, storytelling, poetry, metaphor, folklore and mythology thus constitutes a resource of no small value. If integrated properly with science and technology, it offers a huge competitive advantage. Combining habits of the scientific mind of rationality with the spirituality of Irish mythology, for instance, which is not linear but has a meandering interconnectedness, is ideal for an emerging sustainable age where conversation, interpretation, empathy, meaning and relationships are the most critical innovation resources.

// It's technology married with liberal arts, married with humanities, that yields the results that make our hearts sing.

Steve Jobs, co-founder of computer icon Apple, 2011[54] **//**

The late writer, poet and critic Seán Ó Tuama argued that the best of Ireland's literature in English, from Yeats, Synge, Joyce and Heaney, reflects tensions between English and Irish language patterns in society.[55] The less this tension exists the harder it will be to offer works of originality to the world. A failure to appreciate such distinct resources retards Ireland's creative and innovative potential in the economic sphere just as surely as a lack of more tangible resources.

A healthy, creative, locally-rooted indigenous sector drives innovation and entrepreneurship, while simultaneously preserving and strengthening cultural, natural, human and social capital. These forms of capital, as much as financial and intellectual capital, are bases upon which prosperity, and a successful Irish society, will be built. The exemplary firms we examine throughout this book are catalysts for utilising and integrating resources in inspired, creative ways as they seek to generate the sorts of innovative offerings demanded by a sophisticated and discriminating twenty-first century global market.

Ireland's competitive advantage must be based not on ephemeral advantages easily copied by others (like a low corporate tax rate), but upon inimitable and enduring resources. Such resources are as important as science and technology to Ireland's aspirations to become a 'smart' economy. Bound together by a sense of place, the country's distinct resources – like social capital, inseparable from its cultural traditions and complemented by its natural environment and the creative capacities of its people – constitute the basis for a tangible Irish edge.

// Sustainable development is development that meets the needs of the present without compromising the ability of future generations to meet their own needs.
Brundtland Commission, 1987[56] **//**

However, culture is not the only indigenous resource that is often discounted and ignored. Ireland's unique (even iconic) natural environment is also potentially a huge source of competitive advantage. Sustainable development is the fundamental challenge of the twenty-first century, yet it also represents the century's greatest opportunity for business. At its heart is a different way of defining and understanding human progress and acknowledging that ours is a world of limits. Not solely about efficiency, sustainable or 'green' development is also about the *creation* of economic, social and ecological value. Sustainable innovation gives effect to the vision of a sustainable planet, and Ireland, synonymous with the colour green, ought to be at the forefront of such efforts. As an island nation, Ireland's seas offer bountiful wind and wave energy, as well as fish and seaweed resources. The country is second to none in its potential for year-round food production and possesses a heritage of small-scale, deeply rooted associations with the land going back centuries. Alas, though the country is well-positioned to be a leader here, there is little to suggest this is the case. Nevertheless, there are Irish firms like Bord na Móna and Kingspan which trade on their green credentials while developing products and services that are both innovative and sustainable.

Creating Shared Value

Resourcefulness is key to the creation of shared value, providing both economic value for enterprises and social value for communities and societies. Ireland's sense of cultural identity and distinctiveness, illustrated by its achievements in theatre, literature, art, sport and language, offer inspiration for similar achievements in commerce. In particular, if Ireland is going to foster the creation of an innovative learning or knowledge society, it will need to be inspired by the same sort of turbulent creativity and pioneering self-help that characterised Ireland's cultural renaissance of the late nineteenth century, and by that same sense of a shared national project.

All businesses create products and services for their customers that become experiences. The best businesses create a sort of 'shared value' that is not only good for themselves and their customers, but also redounds to the benefit of society and local communities. This idea, introduced in 2011 by Harvard guru Michael Porter and his colleague Mark Kramer, posits that capitalism needs to reinvent itself to combine both profit and social purpose. In this higher, moral form of capitalism, businesses create social benefits for their communities, and by doing things that are good for society, they assure their own economic success.

So, today's most progressive companies leverage their unique resources and expertise in creating economic value by creating social value. This is what will drive the next wave of innovation and productivity growth in the global economy. Businesses, after all, exist in order to meet societal needs

– the economy should work for the society. In the Ireland of the boom years, of course, it seemed the opposite was true. Most Irish policymakers had (and, sadly, still have) this backwards, believing that society must bend to the needs of the economy. The proposition that creating shared value should be a prime enterprise objective represents a fundamentally different approach and is an underlying theme of this book.

> *ll* [T]he strongest international competitors will often be those that can establish deeper roots in local communities ... Shared value holds the key to unlocking the next wave of innovation and growth. It will also reconnect company success and community success in ways that have been lost in an age of narrow management approaches [and] short-term thinking ...
>
> *Michael Porter and Mark Kramer, academics, Harvard University, 2011*[57] *ll*

This process of shared value creation is demonstrated by the Irish enterprises we highlight in this book; they are rooted in and interdependent with their place, and practice an ethos of stewardship and sustainability. They possess this commitment as an important goal in and of itself, as well as a device to foster organisational success. Such firms are characterised by local ownership and control, assets that are firmly anchored in place, and a reliance on distinctive and often tacit indigenous resources. These enterprises should represent an important component of Ireland's future development strategy.

In studying these enterprises, we were struck by elements many of them share. All seem energised and catalysed – or at least informed – by a deep sense of place. Utilising an admittedly impressionistic lens, we identified a trinity of core elements they use to successfully harness Ireland's unique resources to build competitive advantage, elements like cultural inspiration, creative integration and sustainable innovation. We believe that it is the ability of these exemplary enterprises to balance these elements, driven by the overarching goal of creating shared value through the creation of authentic and distinctively Irish offerings, that makes them truly successful *place-based enterprises*.

Greening Ireland's Enterprises

Michael Collins maintained, as did Thomas Davis, that Ireland's strength depended on balancing the material and spiritual, designing a political, economic and social system in accordance with the Irish character. While W.B. Yeats and Eamonn de Valera felt the material had usurped the spiritual, even Seán Lemass, a great pragmatist not given to fanciful talk, castigated the 'old slave spirit' that needed to be eradicated from the collective Irish psyche, switching the rhetoric of economic self-sufficiency to psychological and imaginative self-sufficiency to drive progress.[58]

The enterprises profiled in this book broadly reflect the very best of Ireland's national image, Brand Ireland. Their offerings are distinctively and authentically Irish, branded with a character that is deeper and more real than the fake Irishness conjured up by some marketing or advertising gurus. Here, again, values and integrity are key; a good 'place brand' means having a firm set of beliefs, a clarity of purpose which drives decisions. Who people are determines how they behave, while how they behave determines how they are perceived. John Fanning offers this aspirational image of Brand Ireland:

❡❡ Ireland is an island nation whose people have had to overcome tremendous adversities from a colonial past before taking their place among the nations of the world. Being forced to continually define their identity in relation to more powerful neighbours provided them with a distinctively holistic world view – a belief that the

pursuit of material prosperity must be accompanied by the pursuit of spiritual prosperity in such a way that they enhance each other. A natural gift for conversation and storytelling inspired by a rich oral and written literary tradition and a vibrant contemporary literary scene make the ideal hosts for the tourist, and natural affinity for counter-intuitive thinking make them ideal participants in today's business world. The Irish look at the world and see it whole, which gives them not only a more balanced perspective on life but a more 'green' perspective on the planet.

John Fanning, Irish brand expert and UCD lecturer, 2011[59] **"**

In recessionary times, those brands that connect deeply and add the most value to customers' lives are set to enjoy the greatest future. Surveys show that, while the past must have modern relevance to maintain its meaning, there is increasing demand for brands that are real, authentic and honest, and which adopt traditional approaches to meet today's needs.[60] This implies a growing celebration of craftsmanship, artisan skills and interest in origin as a mark of quality and trust; this 'passion for place' is Brand Ireland's great opportunity. Small Irish enterprises that specialise in particular crafts, like Bunbury Boards in wooden products, Folláin in fresh fruit preserves, Glenisk in yogurt or Flahavan's in porridge, are doing precisely that.

" [M]any people fear that Ireland's unique emerald landscape and delightfully eccentric culture and identity could get paved over on this road to paradise. This tension now afflicts every modern society, but is particularly acute in places like Ireland, with a robust local culture and environment ... How countries manage this tension is going to be one of the great political dramas of the early 21st century.

Thomas Friedman, New York Times columnist, 2001[61] **"**

Ireland is ideally positioned to capitalise on the emerging trend of sustainable development, yet authenticity must be the source of Brand Ireland's potential. The country needs to develop sufficiently strong cultural and environmental filters to operate successfully in the world. It must sustain and harness those distinctive cultural, natural and social resources that stimulate imagination and creativity, nurture the innovative spirit, promote global citizenship and emphasise ecological and community sustainability. While there is much debate on the need to develop a creative 'knowledge' economy, many seem blind to the valuable role which culture, identity and a sense of place might play. But like physical infrastructure, these need investment too.

Ireland's colonial past has been blamed for 'malignant shame' and a witch's brew of problems: cultural inferiority, suppressed feelings, dependency, substance abuse, irresponsibility, doublethink, duplicity, denial, deference, moral cowardice, bigotry and begrudgery.[62] The boom years have not wiped out the detritus of a postcolonial experience: humiliation, alienation, low self-esteem, failure of the spirit and a weak national identity. Characteristics traceable to a colonial legacy were much in evidence during the Celtic Tiger years, with overindulgent property speculation, overemphasis on foreign direct investment, loss of cultural distinctiveness, marginalisation of the Irish language, environmental degradation and anti-social behaviour. Some suggest the Irish look at nature with colonised minds and deep self-disregard. As poet Joseph Horgan puts it: 'The land is loved, the ownership of it is loved, but it is not valued.'[63] Surely it is time to leave this behind!

I am confident that drawing on our shared strengths and our ethical values we will rebuild a sustainable and strong economy while also at the same time building a just and inclusive society that ensures the participation of all its citizens.

President Michael D. Higgins, 2011[64]

Conclusion

'' Imagination is the beginning of creation. You imagine what you desire; you will what you imagine; and at last you create what you will.

George Bernard Shaw, Irish playwright, 1921[65] **''**

We see an urgent need to rediscover what historian Kevin Whelan calls 'Deep Ireland', with a renewed respect for the vernacular, traditional and distinctive. This kind of spirit drives the GAA and local Tidy Towns committees.[66] In attempting to foster a distinct competitive advantage, Ireland would benefit by drawing on the inspiration of the earlier Revivals. Enterprises, whether they are commercial, non-profit or 'social enterprises' are made up of groups of people, and people are often inspired by culture. This inspiration is vital if Ireland is to discover its way forward. Rooted in place, inspired by cultural revival movements, and innovative in their approaches to the creation of value, place-based enterprises tap into the deep well of Irish iden-tity in an authentic manner. Culture, to these organisations, is not a mere commodity for sale but a dynamic source of competitive advantage – an Irish edge.

It is fascinating to consider where such a marriage of capability, innovation, culture, identity and sense of place might lead. Combining creativity and a self-help ethos could produce development that is rooted in place *and* socially, economically and environmentally sustainable – a nation globally competitive while distinctively Irish. By marrying the global with the local, Ireland has a real opportunity to forge a unique development path.

II

Stories of Distinctively Irish Enterprises

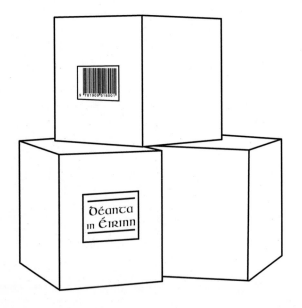

3

Telling Tales

Customers and consumers around the world immediately connect Ireland with the colour green. Many value the country's long, rich history and unique cultural identity (these elements are especially revered in China).
Mary Shelman, Harvard Business School, 2012[1]

Introduction

In Chapter 2 we tangled with the tacit, tough-to-capture factors that enable enterprises to compete on authenticity, character and distinctiveness and capitalise on Ireland's cultural assets. These are the core of the Irish edge and are quite different from more commonly understood factors of production. They work together in complex ways to supply both vision and capability. Ireland, in the past, has often had vision without capability; recently, it had capability without vision. But we believe that both vision and capability are necessary to build a successful society.

The cutting-edge Irish enterprises we focus on encompass apparent contradictions. They reflect a strong sense of place, but are outward-looking and cosmopolitan; they leverage their Irishness, yet relentlessly compete in global markets; they build upon cultural heritage, yet use the latest science and technology; they are driven to succeed, yet in ways that are economically, socially and environmentally sustainable.

❚❚ [T]hink global, act local means one should consider that everything one does has a global impact – so you may act with a certain sense of responsibility.

Dominique Lieb, Swiss owner of Púca Press, 2012[2] ❚❚

Furthermore, the enterprises profiled in this book are all part of the 'real economy', playing their own roles in pursuit of an ideal. This ideal, while decidedly not de Valera's vision, nevertheless represents a worthy, lofty and shared goal. And why shouldn't Ireland's goals be lofty? An economic strategy not founded upon a real vision of a successful society is hollow and superficial. A real vision is based on more than the cold rationality of economic statistics. Despite Ireland's understandable disappointments with its institutions, there are enterprises that are playing their part in a noble national project.

Why Stories?

❚❚ There is still in truth upon these great level plains a people, a community bound together by imaginative possessions, by stories and poems which have grown out of its own life, and by a past of great passions which can still waken the heart to imaginative action.

W.B. Yeats, 1903[3] ❚❚

Although we offer the rudiments of a perspective on, if not a theory of, Irish development, we have no interest in approaching our task in a faux scientific manner. We take a different tack, which is more intuitive and emotional. We rely on the eminently Irish art of storytelling as a vehicle to illustrate the Irish edge. Business academics call such accounts 'case studies', applying to them a sense of objectivity and scientific rigour, but such cases are often no more than stories intended to be instructive or salutary. We simply call them stories here ... stories of Irish place-based enterprises that are inspired by Ireland's culture, demonstrate creativity in imagination and integration, and innovate for the sustainable creation of economic, social and environmental value. Why stories? Stories help us to drill deeply into the rich vein of knowledge and experience found in inspirational ventures. They highlight those elements that make an enterprise – and the products or services it sells – distinctive or unique. Every product, after all, tells its own story. The time has come for those products designed with sustainability, efficiency and functionality in mind, and the imaginative entrepreneurs who created them, to be heard. Stories illustrate our argument that culture and sense of place represent meaningful resources that can be harnessed for competitive advantage. They are pigments in a larger social and economic picture.

Good stories are grounded and personal, intimate and illuminating, creative and inspirational. A good story, as the old saw goes, can 'shorten the road' with its winding digressions. In a good story the destination is less important than the journey itself.

Indeed, there are many inspiring stories that sit squarely at the intersection of Irish culture and commerce. Ireland has always been a land of imagination, though this has often been unharnessed or disconnected from reality on the ground. Yet, there are many successful Irish enterprises that have tapped into this rich trove of the imagination, integrating it into a variety of world-class products and services.

Of course, these enterprises are neither perfect nor reflect an elect. It is a risky business at best to choose exemplars; enterprises change, and even fail, in unanticipated ways and at unexpected times. Besides embarrassment, such failures provoke questioning. One need look no further than the fate of some of the firms highlighted by *In Search of Excellence*, Tom Peters' and Robert H. Waterman's path-breaking business book published in 1982. We acknowledge that, perhaps, some of the enterprises discussed in this book will fail before our work is even published. But in a world of relentless flux and challenge, where firms, markets and environments change constantly, how could this *not* happen? We think it worth the risk.

But we do hedge our bets. We have not selected exemplars to present idealised, all-encompassing prototypes of some pseudo *uber-Gaelic* enterprise. Rather, we have selected those businesses that demonstrate, at least at a point in time, key attributes important to the development of indigenous enterprise and an economy appropriate to Irish aspirations. Most are small to medium-sized ventures. Some are non-profit or social enterprises. All draw on native resources, both cultural and natural, as they leverage in diverse ways Ireland's distinctive heritage. Many demonstrate stewardship of bountiful natural capital and help to cultivate Ireland's 'green' image. Rooted at home, some are nevertheless global players in cutting-edge industries; others create value from native resources, producing traditional products and evincing a tangible sense of place. Many are quite successful in meeting the objectives of the 'triple bottom line'. They are profitable, produce socially-beneficial outcomes, and protect Ireland's natural capital, all of which helps facilitate the creation and sustenance of a successful society.

The challenge, of course, is to reinterpret tradition and culture for a digital age and experience economy. Ireland's distinctive cultural heritage, unappreciated or trivialised as it often is, represents a significant asset and, potentially, a core source of global advantage. Indeed, this was the theme of our previous book.[4] Yet, this generated several obvious, logical questions, like what does such an approach actually look like in practice, and what are some examples of enterprises that exemplify this? This book attempts to address these questions.

The stories we recount provide a glimpse, a taste, a hint of what might be: a flourishing Irish economy, leavened with a significant number of globally-competitive indigenous enterprises, embedded in and serving a successful Irish society. These enterprises add balance, rooted as they are in physical and cultural place; they reflect the mirror opposite of those enterprises that are no more than temporary expedients, useful instruments of the global economy's invisible hand. This book makes a start at telling their stories. And like most good stories, ours rarely run in straight lines, and few are as simple as they first appear.

Introductory Tales

Our stories are about authentic and distinctive experiences: a reason three hundred thousand people from all over the world, mostly young, are drawn to Fleadh Cheoil na hÉireann, a ten-day event organised by Comhaltas Ceoltóirí Éireann, which embraces Irish cultural traditions, music, song, dance and language. Or Scoil Samhraidh Willie Clancy (Willie Clancy Summer School), Ireland's largest traditional music summer school held every July in Miltown Malbay, County Clare in memory of piper Willie Clancy. With master classes and concerts held by the most accomplished traditional artists, it attracts a cosmopolitan, global mix spilling out from pubs on to the streets.

Yet, even with such successes, and many more besides, modern Ireland is often dismissive of culture, except as a product to be hawked to tourists. Some see Irish culture as a retrograde idea, a backward-looking anachronism replete with rural idylls, religious dogma and frugal comfort. Many still use the phrase 'diddly-eye' to refer to traditional music, as if it is beneath contempt. This about an artistic form true to its roots, adaptable to – but not overwhelmed by – outside forces, and acclaimed internationally for its skill, authenticity and integrity.

A dearth of national self-confidence is well illustrated by the knee-jerk reaction to the establishment of the National Leprechaun Museum. Located in Dublin's city centre, the museum introduces the leprechaun and other creatures from folklore and mythology in a fun and engaging way. But it is *not* what you think! No exercise in Paddywhackery, it is fun and light-hearted but not patronising, cheesy or tacky, and very light on kitsch. The creation of leading furniture designer Tom O'Rahilly, the museum is an interactive experience that encompasses the best of Irish folklore, essentially exploring cultural identity through imagination, poetry and story-telling.

> For thousands of years, our forebears retold and refined these stories on this island; we should not forget such rich oral traditions. These stories are coloured by the landscape, our collective memories and our natural inclinations.
>
> Tom O'Rahilly, founder of the National Leprechaun
> Museum, 2012[5]

Of course many Irish are sceptical. One newspaper scoffed: 'Admission: one pot of gold, to be sure and *begorrah.*'[6] Another had this barb: 'It's a little hard to believe there is going to be such demand for visits to a museum dedicated to something that does not actually exist. Well, put it this way – have you ever laid eyes on a leprechaun?'[7] A Tourism Ireland source sniffed: 'It is a derogatory symbol from an Irish perspective.'[8]

Luckily, not everyone agrees. New York-born journalist Margaret E. Ward, who moved to Ireland in 1995, condemns the 'po-faced indignation about the image of "modern" Ireland.'[9] She argues that the museum is the kind of humorous initiative people should welcome, challenging those who raise their eyes to heaven when they read about the museum. When many Americans visit Ireland they find a little of the heritage they seek in fairy forts dotted around the country, and in the Celtic crosses, folklore and friendliness they encounter from time to time. Like us, Ward believes

Ireland won't grow tourism by trying to sell something everyone else has (and often does better).

An inspiring Irish story tied to a distinctive place is always a great seller. Take, for instance, Fragrances of Ireland, based in Kilmacanogue, County Wicklow. It is a rarity in the fragrance industry: an independent Irish perfume house. Established in 1983, the company uses vivid images and colours, poetry and a distinctively Irish identity to promote its best known brand, 'Inis'. While the flowers from which the company's perfumes are distilled (such as lavender) are not uniquely Irish, and clearly scent plays a significant role in any decision to purchase perfume, a great draw for customers is the story the company is selling. Its inspirational products, Managing Director David Cox says, 'tell beautiful and captivating stories which transport the senses of customers to magical places where they experience the sensual feel of Irish nature.'[10]

Nor does the value of Irishness only hold true for small or craft-based enterprises. Some global leaders – important players in the 'real' economy – also leverage their Irishness. Take Paddy Power, for example; the success of this innovative bookmaker has much to do with a culture of horse trading deep in the Irish DNA. Or Barry's Tea; its distinctive 'nostalgia' advertising offers a neatly integrated blend of history, tradition, quality and cosmopolitanism. Set up in 1901 and still based in Cork City, Barry's Tea remains in family hands. We have US friends who, having been to Ireland, refuse to drink the 'dishwater' at home and confine themselves to Barry's Tea for those 'golden moments'.

Or take the Boyne Valley Group, another family business that has stood the test of time. Founded by Malachy McCloskey in 1958 and now spanning thirty-three categories of branded food, personal care and household products, it has deep roots in Drogheda, County Louth. Although not a business that caters to cultural tourists, Boyne Valley nevertheless demonstrates a profound sense of place. It seems, at first glance, rather incongruous, but it publishes and markets books on the history, culture and natural environment of its region. These are not designed to entice customers to buy more of its products; they are works of obvious quality, deeply related to the Boyne Valley. This is more than a novelty: it is an emotional expression of something that deeply matters to the community in which the enterprise is embedded.

▐▐ In a real way a mill binds a community together and I do not think that it is too fanciful to say that a mill is also a symbol. It is a symbol of husbandry, of nurturing and above all of peace and harmony in the contract between man and the good earth.

Malachy McCloskey, founder of the Boyne Valley Group, 2005[11] *▐▐*

Overview of Stories

Unfortunately, we cannot tell *every* story but must confine ourselves to a select few to illuminate our core thesis. All use distinctive Irish resources to produce globally competitive goods or services leading to meaningful experiences rooted in an authentic sense of place. We have concentrated on a number of key sectors where our evidence shows the country can best leverage its Irish edge, as follows:

- Chapter 4, A Place in the Heart, focuses on tourism and travel, highlighting the inspiring story of Cnoc Suain, a historic, pre-famine hill village of two hundred acres of pristine wilderness in Connemara. This enterprise sets a new and higher bar for Irish tourism ventures.
- In Chapter 5, Keeping the Tradition Alive, we look at enterprises in the arts and media sector, such as the Irish World Academy of Music and Dance, the Other Voices music festival, and animation and television production

company Telegael, which leverage Ireland's great story-telling traditions using a modern format.

- Chapter 6, Making Sense (Not 'Stuff'), covers craft and design, drawing on Ireland's heritage of imagination to create authentic experiences. Brian de Staic, one of the country's foremost jewellery designers; Louis Mulcahy, Ireland's most famous potter; and the Wild Goose Studio, where artisans craft unique artefacts based upon Irish myths and history, show how tradition and modernity work in perfect harmony to fashion unique items.

- In Chapter 7, The Green Island, we examine some of Ireland's food enterprises, such as that great example of Irish global branding, Kerrygold, as well as artisan food enterprises, such as the Nenagh-based Country Choice Shop and Café and Cork-based Folláin, a maker of traditional Irish preserves.

- Ireland also possesses a long tradition of brewing and distilling, and in Chapter 8, The Independent Spirit of Ireland, we describe the fascinating story of whiskey upstart Cooley Distillery and its innovative yet traditional offerings.

- Some may feel we only feature enterprises that are too small and neither scalable nor likely to be, but we disagree. In Chapter 9, Sustainable but Scalable, we look at several sizeable Irish enterprises, especially small green ventures with potential to develop a global presence. We describe a hugely successful indigenous venture that never forgets its roots, the Kerry Group. Though only founded in the 1970s, the Kerry Group is now a major global player in a number of food industry segments.

Conclusion

Human beings express themselves with their stories; it is no less so for organisations. While the following narratives describe just a few enterprises we have chosen from the many inspirational companies operating in Ireland, they are vivid and salutary. They offer some evidence that the advice we proffer has legs, that it is practical and achievable rather than romantic or pie-in-the-sky. We are reminded of a tale, perhaps apocryphal, concerning the late Taoiseach Garrett FitzGerald. An academic, he was fond of theorising. Once, while seated at the Cabinet table, he is said to have asked, 'Well, that works alright in practice, but does it work in theory?'

As you read the following stories, you may have a similar reaction. We modestly hope our tales will spur questioning and conversation over both the theory and practice of Irish economic development. Frankly, it is difficult for us to get too excited about Ireland's low corporate tax rate. The real action and excitement in Ireland, we believe, centres on enterprises like those now described. Much can be learned from their stories.

4

A Place in the Heart – Tourism and Travel

Cnoc Suain is not preserving Irish language, music, traditions and crafts to enshrine them. This is no theme park; it is a place of living culture, oozing with pride and determination to share some of the joys of its heritage.

Irish Times, 2008[1]

Background

At 10 years of age Charlie Troy sat at the kitchen table of his home in a South Dublin housing estate and drew a picture of a small cottage on a hill, surrounded by a lake, river and mountains. He told his mother, 'Someday I'm going to live there!' Meanwhile, at the opposite end of Ireland, Dearbhaill Standún was growing up in the wilds of Connemara, fully immersed in the beauty of that unique place. This was the beginning of a dream for this special couple. But it was not a dream alone, for over time they developed a vision to see and shape it and the determination to make it a reality.

The couple first met while Dearbhaill was teaching in Dublin, but she always had a strong sense that she would someday head back to the West, buy a farm, and live a rural lifestyle. Eventually, they both found their way to Galway, where they married, had three children, and built a home in An Spidéal (Spiddal).

If Charlie and Dearbhaill's story had been conjured up by Hollywood, perhaps it would have had a variant of that line from *Field of Dreams*: 'If you build it, they will come.' But life rarely follows a Hollywood script. It has taken Charlie and Dearbhaill well over a decade of struggle to make the dream of Cnoc Suain a reality. Widely acknowledged as emblematic of the very best in the Irish tourism sector, Cnoc Suain is a *living* and a *real* place – an environment, enterprise and experience awash with integrity.

❝ [Cnoc Suain is] serving as a trailblazer and a power-house in promoting sustainability and mindfulness of the earth's – and mankind's – precious resources.

Travel + Leisure *magazine, 2010*[2] **❞**

Located outside of An Spidéal, Cnoc Suain is a restored seventeenth-century hill village that celebrates a people, place and heritage. Its core mission is to 'present Irish culture, nature and heritage with the sophistication and high standard which befits it, without compromising its integrity and authenticity.'[3] Indeed, integrity and authenticity are integral to the very idea of Cnoc Suain and are everywhere in evidence, even in the smallest details.

Unobtrusively located in the middle of a windblown Connemara bog, Cnoc Suain, translated as 'peaceful hill', is firmly tethered to its native place, as much a part of the landscape as the bog that surrounds it. It is an enterprise that generates value through creating authentic experiences for its guests, who can explore the rich life of a Connemara bog, learn a *céilí* dance, or immerse themselves in local music and poetry. All these experiences are fed by an intense connection with the natural surroundings and with the traditions, cultural heritage and history of Connemara. Cnoc Suain taps into the emotional core of those who visit it, creating the conditions for experiences that are often transformative. These experiences are visceral and emotional; it is, after all, what we *feel* that is more likely to change us than what we *know*.

Clearly out of step with the mainstream tourism sector, Cnoc Suain does not offer plastic shillelaghs, 'Kiss me I'm Irish' buttons or other forms of Paddywhackery. Rather, it creates experiences that are unique and authentic, but, admittedly, not for everybody. Infused with a palpable sense of place, Cnoc Suain is developing a growing programme of experiences for discriminating visitors in search of mean-ingful engagement with the traditions, culture, language and natural wonders of Connemara. These experiences are provided through half-day cultural programmes, folkloric evenings and longer residential programmes like the 'Bog and Beach Experience' which combines exploration of the natural history and archaeology of Connemara with song, dance, storytelling, crafting and dining on local foods. Cnoc Suain is a special place where emotional experiences are possible, and where hearts may be moved.

// We never considered cutting corners. Even at our low points, there was never a question of compromising the 'offering'. If it was not working we adapted and adjusted – but never at the expense of the integrity of the entire project. We simply could not do that.

Dearbhaill Standún, 2012[4] *//*

Dearbhaill Standún was long established in the area surrounding Cnoc Suain; her parents founded a renowned craft store in An Spidéal in 1946, and later developed a pioneering hand-crafted knitting industry, exporting Aran sweaters to prime New York stores such as Saks and Lord & Taylor. The Standúns provided much-needed local and national employment through a cottage-industry system where up to seven hundred women plied hand-knitting skills in their own homes. Dearbhaill remembers a business that was something more than that:

❝ Supporting Irish goods was of the upmost importance to my parents. They believed in the quality and value of what we had around us – the culture, landscape and produce. They were also convinced that others would appreciate their uniqueness and richness – once they were introduced to them. As the tourism side of the business developed and bus coaches began to call, the customers, on having completed their purchase, would frequently and spontaneously be invited into the kitchen and given a complimentary cup of tea and sandwich before being entertained to traditional music, with my mother on piano and my brother and I on fiddles – a 'thank you' to the customer and, for us, an opportunity to entertain.

Our home was at the store, with only an unlocked sliding door separating the two. This was symbolic, because home life, business, culture and entertainment all seemed to go hand in hand, blending seamlessly. Even by day our house was buzzing with people – family, staff (who lived with us), neighbours and customers, while at night it was alive with music. Groups such as the Clancy Brothers, Wolfe Tones, the Dubliners, members of the Chieftains and many more, as well as local sean-nós singers and musician friends, would drop in, and it would be music till morning – maybe 7 a.m.! Then the sliding door would open, and it would be business as usual.

Dearbhaill Standún, 2012[5] *❞*

Dearbhaill, herself an accomplished fiddler, is a founding member of the traditional music group Dordán, acclaimed for its distinctive mix of Irish traditional and baroque music. Dearbhaill's background and experiences in culture, education and musical entertainment imbue her with a rich appreciation of and commitment to the Irish language, music and culture, particularly that of her native Connemara.

Charlie, on the other hand, grew up in the south Dublin suburb of Walkinstown, in one of the housing estates that sprang up in the late 1940s and early 1950s. But with the farm fields outside his back door still stretching uninterrupted to the Dublin mountains, he had ample opportunity to spend weekends and long summer months outdoors, exploring the countryside, helping his father cut and save the turf, and developing a profound love of nature. He grew up in a home which featured a genuine interest in Irish culture and politics, attended the only Irish-speaking school in Dublin at the time (Coláiste Mhuire on Parnell Square), and engaged in that ritual shared with so many other young Irish: attending summer college in the Gaeltacht. It was no surprise that Charlie, like Dearbhaill, became a teacher. A fluent Irish speaker and environmental scientist, he is deeply interested in the natural history and archaeology of Connemara. Celebrated writer and naturalist Michael Viney calls him 'a tireless disciple of natural Connemara – animal, vegetable or mineral.'[6] Indeed, both Charlie and Dearbhaill are disciples of a cultural and a natural cause, fostering an ethos of learning that permeates Cnoc Suain.

// Education is at the heart of it, in the sense of sharing knowledge in a creative and joyous way.

Dearbhaill Standún, 2012[7] **//**

Nevertheless, Cnoc Suain is also a commercial enterprise that must, at a minimum, pay its way. Fortunately, in an increasingly globalised economy, with its evolving interest in authentic experiences, significant opportunities exist for indigenous enterprises like Cnoc Suain that marry traditional skills and quality, leveraging these with a contemporary commitment to excellence and service. Yet, embarking on such a strategy also requires no little risk-taking, a healthy dose of creativity and innovation, and an entrepreneurial bent – the willingness to try what has not been done before. It took an abiding belief in the idea, and a tremendous financial, physical and emotional investment. Few would have seen a way to make the dream of owning and running a place like Cnoc Suain a reality, and fewer still would have had the faith, persistence and sheer tenacity to give it effect. Or, put less delicately, few would be crazy enough to do it!

❙❙ The exhaustion, fear, anxiety, worry, feelings of isolation and self-doubt – 'Everyone knows we are crazy but they don't want to say it!' Deep down we didn't doubt the concept, but we asked ourselves, 'Why did it have to be us?'

Dearbhaill Standún, 2012[8] **❚❚**

The Evolution of a Dream

Luckily, this extraordinary couple was not lacking in skills, energy and chutzpah. Cnoc Suain was and remains a risky endeavour in commercial terms and, like most entrepreneurial ventures, a demanding one in personal terms. But for its owners, it is also a labour of love – and love has a way of generating passion, enthusiasm and energy.

There was no dramatic epiphany, but over the course of time these two teachers began to dream of restoring an old cottage as a sort of 'cultural retreat' to nurture and share in an authentic way the vibrant local culture and magnificent natural environment with both overseas and Irish visitors. They were not able to act on this for a long time, but the idea gestated and, finally, in 1995 they purchased an old farm north of An Spidéal, about a mile away from where they were living. It provided more than a lone cottage, but an entire old village in need of restoration.

❙❙ Charlie remembered a place on one hundred and ninety acres that had been for sale a few years before ... he also remembered the name of the auctioneer and phoned him. The auctioneer thought it was still for sale, but that the owner was living in the US. He told us to hop over the gate and have a look. We did that and, as we strolled up the pathway, we could not believe what was unfolding with each step we took. To this day, seventeen years on, we have to remind each other of how people are seeing it as *they* approach for the first time.

It was magical. I could not believe that I had lived all those years in Spiddal – two miles down the road – without knowing that such a place existed. As we came to the bottom of the hill and saw the old thatched cottage just ahead of us, the whole place felt as if someone had wrapped it in a shroud and that it had been like this for years and years – a secret place that encapsulated, for me, everything I had grown up with. The closer we got to the top of the hill, the more amazing it seemed, with a 360° spectacular view over lake, river, mountains and sea. In one way it seemed like a ghost ship, with everything there, and a stillness and sense of timelessness, holding within it the story of our past. We were speechless.

We found out that the owner was actually at home but not there that evening. The following morning we came again to meet him and that evening took our three daughters to see the place. They were 13, 9 and 7 years of age. I have to admit I used a bit of psychology on them – saying to Charlie that we should tell them we were looking at a 'farm', which immediately conjured up images of Connemara ponies, etc. It worked and they were very excited when they saw it. We told the owner there and then that we would buy it.

Dearbhaill Standún, 2012[9] **"**

They began the work of restoration on a part-time basis in 1996, initially with the help of a local builder. However, with the Celtic Tiger's booming economy in full flight, it was not easy to find tradesmen, so they did a lot of the work themselves. They had always known it was going to be difficult; it was a good thing they had little idea *how* difficult it would be.

❰❰ The restoration work was emotionally, physically and financially draining; we were also raising a family of three girls. But all the time we felt it would come out right; we believed in what we were doing, although at times we questioned our own sanity! Sometimes, one of us would feel like putting up the 'For Sale' sign on the farm gate, out of pure exhaustion or because of that 'sinking' feeling, but the other would carry the load for that brief period.

Charlie Troy, 2012[10] **❱❱**

Cnoc Suain evolved from a dream to a vision, to an all-consuming project, in which Charlie and Dearbhaill were fully invested at every conceivable level, and in a very hands-on way. They invested *all* their own money and emotions into this life-project and raised additional funds through the sale of some property and through loans from family and friends – not to mention their own 'sweat equity'. They tried to avoid bank credit as much as possible. In 2001, Charlie took a five-year career break in order to fully devote himself to the restoration effort. The restoration was to be not only authentic but also sustainable, with renewable energy and profound attention to its sense of place.

With the dearth of trade workers, the reconstruction of the stone cottages presented a particular challenge: skills in working with stone in the traditional way were in short supply. Fortunately, Dan and Serban, two Romanians who had been working in a joinery firm in An Spidéal and knew something about stone-working, lent their skills to the effort. There was something of a commune about it as they all shared the place and common endeavour: the family, the Romanian workers, a number of dogs, Connemara ponies and some sheep and cattle. Gradually, what had been ruins, little more than stone bothies (basic shelters) deserted by their inhabitants more than a century ago and gradually being reclaimed by the land, were renovated to a high modern standard. The thatched and slate-roofed stone cottages on the property, some dating back to 1691, now incorporate modern conveniences (discretely) for the comfort of guests, while offering a level of peace, tranquillity, comfort and ease not easily found in contemporary, globalised Ireland. Sited in a place of natural wonders and cultural inspiration, married to carefully chosen modern amenities (but without distractions like television), the cottages retain the simple elegance and integrity of their heritage, fitting effortlessly into their own physical landscape, solidly anchored in their place. They breathe a sense of permanence and possess a real identity.

Meeting the Marketplace

After intense effort, Cnoc Suain now represents something unique in Ireland: an authentically restored hill village or *clachán*. Most of the land is moor and bog, gradually descending on one slope to a forest and lake. It is a Special Area of Conservation (SAC), where 'hen harrier, goshawk, merlin and peregrine share enormous and luminous spaces.'[11] Located in an Irish-speaking area steeped in traditional music, song and dance, Cnoc Suain is also well placed for study of the unique flora and fauna of Connemara.

ll Apart from the charm and beauty of the place, it had many advantages in terms of business. It was a wild and beautiful place, on two hundred acres, only a twenty-minute drive from Galway. The entrance was on the main road, on a scenic route on which tour buses travelled. It was in the Gaeltacht, and contained all the elements of the Connemara landscape, habitat and vernacular architecture.

Dearbhaill Standún, 2012[12] *ll*

Yet, just when they thought the hard bit was really behind them, Dearbhaill and Charlie realised that the restoration itself did not present the most difficult challenge. Having accomplished the physical renovation, the ultimate challenge for the couple was to organise the operation of Cnoc Suain as a successful and self-sustaining enterprise. This was difficult, as there was no standard model to follow for the 'business' of generating heritage experiences. And could there ever be a more intangible product? The essential commercial question became: what were Charlie and Dearbhaill selling with Cnoc Suain? What exactly was the product? Perhaps the answer paraphrases the assertion of that other remarkable West of Ireland entrepreneur, Tarlach de Blacam, whose Inis Meáin story we detailed in Chapter 1: 'We don't just sell tourism, we sell tradition, stories and place.'

❝ In hindsight, restoring that first cottage was probably the easiest part of the whole restoration. We realised early on that we were not fitting into any established model. We were not a B&B, a hostel, a hotel, a golf course, or a walking/cycling holiday. Not having a label, a tag that could be slotted into a category, proved to be a problem when it came to getting recognition and funding. We were told by various visitors to Cnoc Suain over the years that we were ten years ahead of our time. It was meant as a compliment, but our hearts sank each time we heard it because it compounded the reality of it all ... There was such frustration at not being recognised and finding yourself listed under 'other' in the tourist listings and categories – side by side with a laundrette and an estate agent, because there was no category for culture.

Dearbhaill Standún, 2012[13] *❞*

Of course, such 'dreaminess' causes marketing problems. How do you market a 'product' that is so nebulous and difficult to pin down? If Cnoc Suain does not fit into any typical tourist industry category, how do you advertise it? The initial thinking had been to promote it as a residential programme, offering customised cultural programmes for private groups and universities, but then fate intervened. In late 2007, just when they were ready to roll out the first residential pilot programmes, a fire consumed the Sean Teach ('Old House') cottage at the centre of the village. The insurance company would not pay out, and with Ireland descending into economic recession, the financial markets had frozen up and there was simply no credit available.

With the Sean Teach out of commission, the residential programmes were put on hold, and Charlie and Dearbhaill had to develop something to bridge the gap and generate some badly-needed income – and quickly. Their solution was to develop a series of one-day cultural experiences as an alternative to the residential immersion programmes that had been planned. These one-day experiences would give visitors a window – a glimpse into Gaelic culture. The trick was to do this in a way that had integrity and character, without descending into either mass-market frivolity or ponderous seriousness. To create the one-day experiences, Dearbhaill and Charlie fell back on their teaching ethos and background, developing programmes that were intended to be original and natural, with equal measures of learning and fun. They drew equally on the area's environmental riches of bogland and seashore, and the community's rich cultural resources of music, dance and poetry.

" We saw a gap in the market – visitors were being whizzed from one 'must see sight' to another without accessing the Irish language, nature, customs, or even the people! We believed the day would come when they would want to know more about these aspects, and we believed that together, we could deliver on this. We had first-hand knowledge of the topics, experience in education and teaching, were hard workers, had tenacity and resilience, and worked well together – most of the time! It seemed a very attractive prospect to earn your living doing what you love.

Dearbhaill Standún, 2012[14] ***"***

Recognition

Dearbhaill and Charlie's plans were shaped by infrastructural limitations. Given the interactive presentation/classroom dimension of the experience, visitors had to be in the same place at the same time; that meant, with the narrow roadway and limited parking capacity, that the programme would have to be targeted at coach tour operators. Also, visitor numbers would have to be strictly limited in order to preserve the 'personal' dimension of the experience. Finally, arrangements were made with a newly-established coach company in Galway to reach visiting groups in Galway City and transport them to Cnoc Suain.

The Old Testament exhorts us to 'cast your bread upon the waters'. In 2008, Dearbhaill and Charlie did just that, launching the day programmes into a very uncertain market, at a time of deepening economic distress. With declining tourist numbers, tour operators were loath to experiment and tended to stick with the old reliables, so initial progress was slow. Yet, Cnoc Suain represented something that was virtually unknown in the Irish tourism market, and began to win a succession of prestigious awards. These awards helped to turn things around, giving Cnoc Suain legitimacy and credibility within the industry. Good things began to happen, including winning a contract with a major high-end US tour operator, Tauck Tours, for inclusion in its 'Best of Ireland Tour'.

❮❮ Recognition did come eventually – the Galway County Council's Connemara Heritage Award, a two-page spread in *The Guardian* newspaper, followed by a World Ethical Travel Award and inclusion in their Green Travel List, and, finally, in November 2010 we received a Global Vision Award from *Travel + Leisure* magazine, the only business in Europe to receive one that year. These awards helped us enormously, not only from a business perspective, but

as confirmation that we were not, after all, totally crazy in our thinking and that this was, in fact, the way to go.

Dearbhaill Standún, 2012[15]

Transformative Experiences

Inspired by its setting in the spectacular, ancient landscape of West Galway, Cnoc Suain's philosophy is to preserve this pristine natural environment while nurturing the unique culture and traditions of Connemara. Cnoc Suain is a dynamic, living place; it is not a museum. Visitors participate in programmes of various lengths and are encouraged to be actively engaged rather than mere passive observers. Activities include Irish music, song and storytelling; a walk in the bog; workshops on local flora and fauna; a *céilí* dance; folklore evenings; literary programmes; tin whistle and Irish language workshops; *seisiúin*; and more. Many of these programmes are led by local people, experts who themselves are excited by the opportunity to pass along the cultural and environmental knowledge they have acquired. Charlie and Dearbhaill have created programmes that appeal not only to the Irish diaspora and other overseas visitors, but to the 'native' Irish as well, who visit Cnoc Suain to re-ground themselves in their own traditions and folklore. It is a robustly unique and authentic experience that bears little resemblance to the carefully choreographed and sanitised versions of Irish culture and heritage too often packaged for the consumption of tourists.

❝ I find that visitors are becoming more discerning. They decide to come because they are interested, but they know very soon whether you are the real deal or not. You are connecting people at an emotional level to something, so there is no point in attempting to fake it. It has to come from the heart as well as the head.

Dearbhaill Standún, 2012[16] ❞

The goal is that every visitor's experience at Cnoc Suain will be personal and intimate. Just as visitors bring their own unique life experiences and histories with them, they may be transformed in different ways. So much depends, of course, on what they themselves seek. Cnoc Suain offers a tranquil locale for such learning and reflection, set in a magnificent and inspiring landscape. In offering an experience that will be different for each visitor, it provides the possibility for an experience that none of them will find anywhere else. High-end travel companies have taken note, increasing their visits and willing to pay a premium for an experience that their discriminating clientele values – an experience that is different from the rest. Now several companies are venturing off the beaten track to take the *bóithrín* to Cnoc Suain with their high-end tours.

There are many tales of how Cnoc Suain is a transformative experience for visitors. It seems to touch a universal nerve about tradition and home, irrespective of whether or not people have any Irish blood. Take the example of Iranian-American woman Sima Miska, who wrote:

❝ Dearbhaill, a wonderful storyteller, recited a poem in Gaelic and she taught us steps to a typical Irish folk dance. Such Fun! It is a 'must see' if you are interested in experiencing a unique way of learning about the culture, history and archaeology of this beautiful and fascinating island.
Sima Miska, visitor to Cnoc Suain, 2012[17] **❞**

As we argue in this book, distinctiveness matters. And why shouldn't learning and reflection and, yes, even reverence, be combined with fun? Cnoc Suain is not a static enterprise; it continues to grow and develop. And long may that continue.

❝ From a business perspective, confirmation came from return visitors, something we value very much. It has been a challenge trying to define and market our product, and

I liken it to filling a large sand bucket using a teaspoon – slow, but sure – because when people come and experience it, they do return and often recommend it to their friends. What has been a very special surprise for us has been the positive attitude and response of local people – young and old – in the Connemara region to Cnoc Suain.

Dearbhaill Standún, 2012[18] **"**

The Future

Charlie and Dearbhaill continue to develop the residential programmes, with an emphasis on traditional music, Gaeilge, crafts and ecotourism. The couple's three daughters are now involved with the business to varying degrees, bringing new energy and ideas. Future plans include developing a 'Cultural Campus' within the hill village based on culture and sustainability, initiating several 'green' learning ventures (Cnoc Suain received an Ecotourisim Ireland 'Gold Cert' in 2012), creating an artisan shop selling local craft and food products, and developing an online element.

Based on heritage, rooted in place, Cnoc Suain is nonetheless modern and contemporary, with 'products' that are eminently practical. It is built on a foundation of authenticity, character and integrity; yet it *is* a commercial venture, and it required a business model that would allow it to survive and thrive. To this end, as far as Dearbhaill, Charlie and Cnoc Suain are concerned, flogging poorly choreographed and derivative representations of what passes for an Irish cultural experience to tourists is *not* an option. Difference, integrity and character are what matter. Cnoc Suain provides an inspiring counter-example, in the authentic, place-based experiences it offers.

" We want Cnoc Suain and its experiences and programmes to be viewed as being fresh and contemporary, while being rooted in tradition ... after all, we live this life in

Cnoc Suain and so do the local people who work with us. It is not an interpretive centre, walk-through exhibit, museum, or a place where actors dress up in period costume to do re-enactments. All of these have their part to play in the broad array of tourist offerings, but they are not what we are about.

Charlie Troy, 2012[19] **"**

Characteristically, Cnoc Suain's programmes treat participants with the respect due to those searching for a connection – whether it be a connection with the landscape and the natural world, with their own history, or with the language, music and traditions of a living culture that may or may not be their own. In the best tradition of genuine Irish hospitality, and with the respect due anyone on a journey, Cnoc Suain endeavours to serve the needs of these travellers.

" I still feel as passionate about it all as I did when we first set out, still get that same buzz when sharing it with visitors. And I now realise that, whatever happens – and it is still very challenging out there – we were not crazy after all, and that being authentic will be key to cultural tourism in Ireland for the foreseeable future.

Dearbhaill Standún, 2012[20] **"**

Conclusion

A recent Harvard Business School publication suggested that 'authenticity will be the buzzword of the twenty-first century.'[21] If Ireland ever hopes to make its knowledge economy more than mere rhetoric, it must draw on its distinct, rare and inimitable resources, no matter how 'soft' these may be. In the following chapter, we look at ventures in the art and media sectors which, like Cnoc Suain, do exactly that, straddling the global and local while remaining rooted and authentic, and loaded with character and integrity.

5

Keeping the Tradition Alive – Arts and Media

Whatever space and time mean, place and occasion mean more.
Aldo van Eyck, Dutch architect, 1961[1]

Introduction

It is estimated that dance phenomenon *Riverdance* has been seen live by well over twenty million people in more than thirty countries and four continents, spawning a host of similar spectaculars like *Lord of the Dance, Gaelforce Dance,* and others. Even though purists may frown, and the novelty may have worn off, *Riverdance* has highlighted the global appetite for Irish cultural endeavours.[2] This appetite extends to China, which appears to have an almost obsessive interest in authentic world cultures, especially in its demand for luxury brands.

❝ China has a desperate need of the past. It is really important to [the Chinese] to find something that is authentic – they want to go back to original roots.
Michele Norsa, Managing Director of Italian luxury goods company Salvatore Ferragamo, 2010[3] **❞**

The huge success of *Riverdance* in China highlights this desire for authenticity. *Irish Times* journalist Fintan O'Toole suspects the dance resonates there because its mass choreography and visual storytelling connect with Chinese memories.[4] The image of the river rolling endlessly onwards, the dance's central metaphor, offers parallels for China's own history. O'Toole reckons that the Chinese identify with Ireland in a way that seems utterly implausible given the huge disparity in population and size. But the Chinese think of themselves as a small nation, bullied and humiliated by more powerful countries. They see in *Riverdance* a moral tale of an oppressed 'great nation' enduring long enough to come into its own. The other great attraction, O'Toole writes, is the show's upbeat take on tradition and globalisation. With its narrative of survival across the millennia, *Riverdance* applies a soothing balm to the Chinese anxiety about the fragility of their own traditions.

In this chapter, using unique stories of enterprising initiatives, we demonstrate how Ireland's traditions in arts and media, whether in music, dance, literature, poetry, drama or storytelling, are more than cultural products. They are distinctive resources that foster the imaginative spirit, stimulate sustainable innovation and develop world-class enterprises. Such cultural resources can provide Ireland with an inimitable competitive advantage – an Irish edge – by mediating between the local and global.

Irish World Academy of Music and Dance

❝ I wanted to affirm that within our individual selves we can reconcile two orders of knowledge which we might call the practical and the poetic; to affirm also that each form of knowledge redresses the other and that the frontier between them is there for the crossing.

Seamus Heaney, Irish poet and Nobel laureate, 2002[5] ❞

Ireland offers a distinctive environment for the traditional arts, illustrated by the Irish World Academy of Music and Dance at the University of Limerick, housed in a building lying on the banks of the Shannon. The river itself is an influential theme, with its mythical origins depicted in a beautiful mural detailing the story of the goddess Sionna. The Academy was founded in 1994 when musician and composer Mícheál Ó Súilleabháin accepted the University's inaugural Chair of Music. It has now grown to nearly three hundred students and sixteen academic programmes. The Academy's artists/scholars-in-residence programme covers classical and traditional music, and contemporary and traditional dance. Participants have included renowned artists such as Breandán de Gallaí, Martin Hayes, Donal Lunny, Jean Butler, Paul Brady and The Chieftains.

The late musician and composer Seán Ó Riada held that Irish traditional music follows a fundamental pattern, differing only by a particular ornamentation. So, a musician who makes variations is a creative contributor to tradition, yet the one who does not is not necessarily a bad musician, merely a passive holder of tradition.[6] When such creative reworking occurs, it has a revitalising effect on the music tradition.[7] Likewise, in the Academy's building, where performance in the arts and academic research sit side by side in an empowering relationship, creativity flourishes. Immersed in music, song and dance experiences, a rich environment is created through the interaction of people sharing ideas and possibilities as they learn from and relate to one another. In forging links between the traditional and the contemporary, the local and the global, the Academy builds upon Ireland's vibrant traditions in music and dance.

With over six hundred graduates to date from forty countries, the Academy offers a rich context for students to experiment with both Irish traditions and their own received traditions, to find their unique voices. International students bring their own musical customs, building upon and enhancing the experiences of their fellow students and gaining in turn a heightened appreciation of their own uniqueness through exposure to Ireland's cultural riches.

Studying in Ireland, redolent still of a distinct sense of place, students both change and are changed. Without doubt, the Academy makes a great contribution to the challenge of cultural globalisation, to the celebration of difference and to the inherent belief in a shared humanity.

Seamus Heaney once said: 'We should keep our feet on the ground to signify that nothing is beneath us, but we should also lift up our eyes to say nothing is beyond us.'[8] Individuals experience the world through their bodies, when hearts as well as minds are engaged, and interpretation is balanced with analysis. While working in the performing arts, students are inspired to receive meaning through their actions, which helps them understand more about themselves. Self-reflection and highly developed hand and body skills foster identity, spurring imagination and the creative spirit.[9] Improvisation in music shares many of the characteristics of complexity in business. What students *know* cannot easily be separated from how they *act*, as they learn best by active engagement in and reflection on practice. Such exposure helps them become self-discoverers; they learn to 'create themselves', the best definition of education we know.

So, with ritual and tradition central to the Academy's programmes, there is likely to be increased demand for its graduates, even in businesses, as organisations seek individuals who can create meaningful products and services without diluting the essential artistic integrity of the creative process. The Academy is in the vanguard with its adventuresome approach to learning, with positive implications for stimulating innovation throughout society. This suggests that the orthodox view is back to front: Ireland's prospects of becoming a 'knowledge' economy would be enhanced if conventional science and technology programmes looked more like those of the Academy. As renowned critic Herbert Read held, the aim of *all* education should be the preparation of artists; he knew such individuals do everything well.[10]

Other Voices

There are other paradigm-shifting, place-based enterprises founded on the arts, such as the Other Voices music festival held each year in Dingle, County Kerry. For the past nine years, music producer, songwriter and broadcaster Philip King has organised this week-long music festival, bringing major international acts to Dingle in early December, filling every hotel room in the area, and providing television content which is transmitted throughout the world. Writer Joseph O'Connor cites Other Voices as a fascinating model of how to bring together culture, cutting-edge technology, innovation and landscape.[11] He sees the festival as an ideal way for Ireland to realise the extraordinary resources it possesses, showcasing them to the world.

King regards imagination as the greatest Irish resource, explaining: 'Other Voices has been a very difficult but very rewarding journey. It's a place of convergence, where tradition, translation and transmission come together.'[12] He says:

// The imagination informs the music, but also the technological development. It's like an artistic pursuit. Irish music has always collided with technology and that collision has affected the artistic process. When Irish music went to America first, it met technology. Records were made and sent home, and we listened to them and copied them. Technology changed our oral transmission of music. That indelible print of the technology is there. It's about trying to find that balance between culture and technology that enables it to be transmitted to the world.

Philip King, 2011[13] *//*

Dingle itself is a special place. Dominated by the sea, the local community values both the diversity of visitors and its own rich language and musical traditions. Other Voices provides live streams of some of the world's hottest acts from tiny, two-hundred-year-old St. James's Church to venues around the town. While the church audience is only about seventy in all, many others watch the performances in local pubs, on laptops, smartphones and other electronic devices. High-definition technology is supplied by high-tech company Intune Networks, yet Other Voices retains the feel of a small traditional music *seisiún*. The combination of technology and tradition, the local and the global, creates a unique experience for artists and audiences. At the same time, Dingle itself weaves its own special magic on participants and audience members alike; coming to this place at the edge of Europe, even for many who've never been before, often seems more like a homecoming than a visit. What could be more inspiring than such a milieu of music, technology, sense of place and spirit?

❛❛ From a small room, in a church, in a little town at the edge of the Atlantic, on the furthermost peninsula in Europe … we can take this message across the world. Through the medium of music and with the technology to transport that, we ultimately retain a sense of who we really are and what we may ultimately become.

Philip King, 2010[14] *❜❜*

Burren College of Art

The Burren College of Art at Newtown Castle, situated just outside Ballyvaughan in County Clare, is also breaking the mould. Located on Ireland's Atlantic seaboard, in the heart of the Burren, a place unlike any other in Ireland, it provides time, space and inspiration for arts education embedded within a unique landscape. The name 'Burren', derived from the Irish word '*Boireann*', means 'rocky place'.[15] An area of 160 square km, the Burren covers parts of north County Clare and south County Galway. Centuries of weathering has produced a terrain of fissured limestone pavements, disappearing lakes, terraced mountains and underground cave systems. The area is famous for its amazing foliage and for containing over five hundred ring forts and eighty Neolithic tombs.

II The Burren is the soul of Ireland – indefinable, elusive but deep-down special. It is our greatest repository of natural and cultural heritage, and encapsulates our very essence as a people.
Brendan Dunford, co-founder of Burrenbeo conservation project, 2011[16] *II*

Set up in 1994 by current College President Mary Hawkes-Greene (and her late husband Michael), the Burren College of Art's location is core to its work as a place-based enterprise. It is a 'hothouse for universal creativity based on Joseph Beuy's belief that "everyone is an artist", meaning "everyone has the capacity to be creative in everything they do".'[17] In practice, this involves the transferability of creative skills and practice to other disciplines and is manifest in the College's role as a catalyst for creative thinking. The Burren provides a rich context that connects the artist's insight with the wider world. Such connectedness makes perfect sense since most of the students come from abroad and, as with the Irish World Academy of Music and Dance, the College's Irish roots are fertilised by ideas from other cultures, and vice versa.

While we do not suggest that culture is a commodity to be monetised, neither do we argue that it explains every-thing (and therefore nothing). Rather, Ireland's unique and distinctive culture represents ways of thinking, practices and beliefs that are products of a shared history and experience. This will assume increasing importance in the emerging economy where innovation and international competitive-ness depend greatly on intangible assets like imagination, intuition and inspiration.

Yet, culture, writ large, does not itself represent a competi-tive resource. In other words, our argument is not that Irish culture per se produces people who are more entrepreneurial, creative or efficient, but certain facets or dimensions of the culture represent resources that can be harnessed to create value, which leads to competitive advantage. For instance, it is generally accepted that dynamic multilingual communities are more likely than monolingual ones to stimulate new ideas and innovation. Ireland possesses a unique linguistic history which can foster world-class ventures in communications and media. Telegael is one such venture.

Telegael

Telegael's motto is 'Fréamhaithe anseo ... ag síneadh amach ar fud an domhain,' or 'rooted in the Gaeltacht ... reaching out to the world.'[18] It operates one of Ireland's largest and most modern television, film and animation studios, employing one hundred full-time staff and up to two hundred others on a contract and seasonal basis. Established in 1988 in An Spidéal in the Galway Gaeltacht, where it remains headquartered today, it also has offices in Los Angeles and London. Telegael develops and produces its own productions but also collaborates with international broadcasters, producers and distributors to produce and finance high-quality children's animation and live-action television productions. Amongst its production partners are Disney, the Cartoon Network, Discovery Kids, the BBC, Nickelodeon, PBS Sprout, ZDF, ABC, the Jim Henson Company, France Television, TG4 and ITV.[19] Telegael productions have been distributed to over one hundred and forty countries and translated into more than forty languages. The company is internationally recognised for its expertise, creativity and production capabilities, with seven Emmy nominations and two Emmy awards amongst its many international accolades.

Telegael's workforce is predominately under 35 years of age and drawn from varied professional, cultural and linguistic backgrounds. This contributes to creativity and makes for a most interesting workplace. The company's expansion is based on significant financial investment in a comprehensive range of up-to-date production and studio facilities and equipment. When first established, Telegael was 85 per cent owned by Údarás na Gaeltachta (The Gaeltacht Authority) and RTÉ, with the balance held by management. Following a buyout, the majority shareholding is now held by management, all of who are fluent Irish speakers and (apart from non-executive chairman Dr Tom Hardiman, former Director General of RTÉ) reside in the Gaeltacht.

❙❙ [Board meetings through Irish] is no big issue for us; it's natural and it works for us ... The power of language exists as much in its potency as a unifying force – building and uniting a community as a team – as it does as a means of communication.

Paul Cummins, CEO of Telegael, 2011[20] **❙❙**

Wexford-born CEO Paul Cummins suggests Telegael's ethos may have been seen by some as overly optimistic in the early 1990s, but now over 80 per cent of Telegael's output is produced for the global market and broadcast outside of Ireland. Indeed, Telegael is better known outside of Ireland than at home where, because of its name, its Gaeltacht location and its strong Irish language ethos, it is sometimes confused with the Irish language television broadcaster TG4. The huge advances in the Internet and global telecommunications over recent years have meant that Telegael's geographical location is largely irrelevant to its partners, but the idyllic location of An Spidéal has real work–life benefits for the Telegael team, most of whom live locally.

Cummins pointed out to us that he is a great admirer of the Kerry Group, viewing that company's achievements as a great example of how a rural-based Irish company can prosper in an international market. He is similarly impressed by how Glen Dimplex, the huge electrical heating manufacturer set up by entrepreneur and educational philanthropist Martin Naughton, with Irish headquarters but global operations, has developed cross-cultural capabilities to succeed in the Japanese and Chinese markets. Cummins believes that new technological advancements and growth in emerging economies present huge possibilities for Irish companies, and Ireland's open economy and the creativity of its people represent key ingredients of international success. He holds that Irish businesses operating on an international level need to be innovative, creative and open to new perspectives while remaining faithful to their core cultural values.

// The availability of high-speed broadband allows us to review our projects online and in real time with our partners in Los Angeles, Sydney, India, London, Paris and elsewhere, something which was inconceivable twenty years ago. When our overseas clients visit to view our operations first-hand, they are amazed to see a world-class facility located in a small village looking out over Galway Bay, as opposed to their expectations of us being in a large metropolis.

Paul Cummins, 2011[21] *//*

While Telegael is a standout example, there are others who successfully leverage Ireland's distinct cultural resources and traditions in communications and media to good advantage. While geographically, much of the television production sector is concentrated in and around Dublin, a significant, if unexpected, cluster also exists in the Gaeltacht around Indreabhán, County Galway. This is largely due to the establishment of TG4 and support by Údarás na Gaeltachta for the media sector over the past few decades. A beneficial and harmonious joining together of culture and technology led to the establishment of this cluster. Since the establishment of TG4 in 1996, forty audio visual companies, employing two hundred and twenty full-time and one hundred and eighty part-time workers, have been set up in the region. TG4 acts as a kind of growth pole around which many supporting industries have grown. Yet, the trend in recent years is for firms, as with Telegael, to look more outward. TG4 was no doubt the stimulus in getting these companies off the ground, but it could not support them forever; the only way for them to grow is internationally.[22] While there is no doubt that the embeddedness of the television production cluster around Indreabhán was fundamental to its evolution, the opportunities and threats depend on its ability to balance local and global ties, as Telegael shows.

Irish as Resource

❝ Next to the failure to curb emigration – the factor which more than any other disillusioned so many people with the road which national independence had taken – the greatest tragedy of modern Ireland is surely the failure to revive the Irish language.

Brian Fallon, former art critic of the Irish Times, *1999[23]* *❞*

Even though the stories in this chapter demonstrate the enormous creative potential of Ireland's culture, every year when the Leaving Certificate results are announced, one can anticipate the response. There is much hand wringing and whingeing about low levels of student achievement in science and mathematics, and demands for a new emphasis on these subjects. We have nothing to argue with there. However, often, critics demand that this new emphasis should be delivered by removing Irish from the curriculum. Why, they say, compel students to study an all-but-dead language that few students will ever use in everyday life, when their time could be devoted to mastering 'useful' disciplines that will provide the groundwork for acquiring in-demand skills in technology and the sciences to fill the high-tech jobs being created by multinational investors in Ireland?

The underlying assumption is that Irish offers no practical advantages. Irish is generally perceived as an artefact of a culture and nationality now gone, originally institutionalised through a misplaced ideological zeal with creating a sense of Irishness. Or, it is simply seen as a failed experiment that should at long last be aborted. Either way, knowledge of Irish is seen to serve no purpose, irrelevant to a twenty-first century globalised island economy. Such thinking is short-sighted, and stale ideas must be discarded if a small country like Ireland is ever to successfully compete in the emerging experience economy.

Genuine bilingualism offers great opportunities, as ventures like Telegael illustrate. It increases Irish people's capacity to move between different realities and points of view, to conceptualise in different ways, with enriching and liberating effects on their capacity to deal with a range of social and economic problems. Dynamic multilingual communities, especially those at the interfaces of languages, are more likely to stimulate ideas and innovation than monolingual ones. Such benefits are ignored by, for instance, Tom Garvin, a former professor of politics at UCD, who, while bemoaning the 'smothering capabilities' and limited 'creative capabilities' of Irish, laments the absence of the teaching of citizenship in schools.[24] He can't have it both ways! The raw material of civic virtue, as with innovation, can only take root within a shared sense of place, of 'we-ness', provided through the kind of intellectual underpinnings of the Gaelic League in the years before the foundation of the State.

Conclusion

The stories we tell throughout this book suggest a radical transformation is needed to nurture Irish creativity and innovation. Conventional wisdom holds that Ireland's competitiveness depends on promoting subjects like science, technology, engineering and mathematics.[25] However, the jobs in most demand in future will be those that accomplish what computers *cannot* do.[26] With competitiveness increasingly dependent on intangible resources such as creativity, imagination, emotions, meaning, memory and community, a profound sense of place is crucial. This is best cultivated within an experiential-learning community.

Today's students must be helped to think globally but feel rooted in Ireland, so learning has to emphasise a shared meaning nurtured by experiences. The more practice and experience they have of exploring their inner emotional world, the more confidently they creatively deal with change and open themselves to new possibilities. The hallmark of a quality education is knowledge *enquiry*, not information receipt, driven by self-discovery: *learning to be* rather than *learning about*. It is precisely this kind of education that best stimulates the craft and design-driven enterprises described in the following chapter.

6

Making Sense (Not 'Stuff') – Craft and Design

Life without industry is guilt, and industry without art is brutality.

John Ruskin, English art critic, 1870[1]

Introduction

Ruskin might have added that industry *with* art *and* meaning is *craft*; indeed, artistry and distinctiveness, meaning and creativity, are all fundamental to the very idea of craft. Ireland is blessed with a rich and distinctive craft tradition, from the silver and gold Ardagh chalice to the bronze Cross of Cong, and the gold, silver, copper and amber used in the Tara Brooch. These artefacts display a sophisticated artistry and imaginative capacity for design that once distinguished Ireland among the nations of Europe.

Craft has a major role to play in the Irish economy, although its importance is rarely recognised at official level. The Irish craft sector is vigorous and, yes, even modern, as the stories in this chapter illustrate. Yet, even with conspicuous successes, there remains a tendency to ignore small, indigenous craft enterprises and, worse yet, to marginalise their achievements. After all, they are not the high-profile, sexy, so-called 'smart' industries said to be Ireland's deliverance and favoured by the policy elite. But after the hi-tech firms have come and gone, it is more likely that indigenous firms like these will remain. In their own sector they are building competitive, world-class businesses that utilise Ireland's imaginative resources and demonstrate real commercial potential.

II In the national development plan, the only time the word design is mentioned is in the context of construction. The luxury market is worth [worldwide] €300 billion based on one thing – design – and here we have an intelligent, creative, passionate nation, and did someone say we couldn't have a piece of that?
Brian McGee, head of market development, Crafts Council of Ireland, 2012[2] *JJ*

For all of Ireland's high-profile aspirations to become a knowledge society, it is worth remembering that craft workers represent our very first knowledge workers. Their knowledge is of a different sort, more holistic, encompassing the head and the heart as well as the hands. It is knowledge rooted in history, tradition and culture. Craft, after all, is about the creation of meaning, not the construction of trinkets and baubles; it can offer a glimpse of deeper thoughts, not just a veneer. This is what the stories that follow illustrate so well.

Louis Mulcahy Pottery

The Irish craft sector is thriving, and nowhere more than in the heart of the Kerry Gaeltacht in Corca Dhuibhne on the Dingle Peninsula. The work of potter Louis Mulcahy, onetime RTÉ cameraman, is utterly modern but distinctively Irish. He has been working for 37 years in his Ballyferriter pottery. The pottery, like a hamlet, has a number of buildings constructed to a very high modern standard, based on the style of traditional Blasket Island cottages. It faces the Atlantic, whilst nestling snugly into the hillside at the base of Cruach Mharthain. The pottery and shop, Potadóireacht na Caolóige, employed nearly seventy people up to a few years ago. Due to the recession, the figure has fallen to under thirty, but Mulcahy says that one of the benefits of the downturn is that the company has been forced to reassess and cut out waste which had grown over the years. They are now a leaner, fitter operation and ready to take advantage of any upturn.

// Once or twice a week we are like excited children on Christmas morning as we open the kiln and take out test pieces. More often than not we are disappointed with the samples, but sometimes an experiment works, and we get a beautiful result which we can repeat and fit into our range. Lisbeth [Louis' wife] asked me recently what I would change if I only had six months to live. I thought about it for a while and said 'nothing'. Despite the trauma of the past few recessionary years I could not think of a better way of life.

Louis Mulcahy, 2012[3] **//**

Having won first prize for pottery in the National Crafts Competition in 1975, Mulcahy moved his workshop from Dublin to Kerry. Like many other entrepreneurs, he and Lisbeth left secure employment and invested their savings in a fledgling business. Over the next thirty years, Mulcahy built a unique enterprise, while moving to the forefront of the craft movement. But the couple did more than open a business in a peripheral area: they embraced a way of life. Louis and Danish-born Lisbeth took the time and effort to learn the Irish language, making it a point to speak it in their home and business. Lisbeth herself runs a successful workshop and shop, Siopa na bhFíodóirí, in Dingle. She designs all the woven goods in the shop, where she employs other weavers to make some of the wall hangings on display. The scarves, throws and table linen are woven for her by a friend. Lisbeth's tapestries are hanging in churches, public buildings and Irish embassies around the world.

With son Lasse now General Manager of the pottery, Louis devotes his time to designing and creating prototypes for the production team and making big, sculptural signature pieces, all the time experimenting with glazes and clays. No doubt the constantly changing colours of the local landscape and sea provide a source of inspiration to this master potter, as Louis himself explains:

" [Here] the sea changes [colour] rapidly ... and you'll get the lovely light bluish green closer in, and then you get a very deep green outside, and then you see it going out to blue in the deeper parts. On other days, you'll see it varying from greys to light greens. And then the hills behind us, which are so brown at certain times of the year ... [will be a] nice purple with the heather on them at different times. The most spectacular things of all here are the sunsets, and they are absolutely roaring-red sunsets, varying off into browns, and that is really beautiful. And that's where the colours [in my pottery] have come from I think. Even though I wasn't quite aware of why I thought they were beautiful when we were doing our experiments, it had to be that what I was seeing around me had gone in [to my subconscious].

Louis Mulcahy, 2012[4] *"*

In 2004 Louis, who is also a poet, became the first Irish craftsman to receive an honorary degree from the National University of Ireland, in recognition of his artistic accomplishments and his practical contributions to the economic prosperity of his community. He has certainly achieved his aspiration to produce superb pottery and develop a studio which would leave an indelible mark on the long-term history of Irish handicraft.

Despite its small size, Louis Mulcahy Pottery is a world-class, globally-oriented business. It exports its products internationally, selling to an educated, sophisticated and demanding segment of cognoscenti in an intensely competitive business. And Ballyferriter is no low-wage environment. Mulcahy is competing – and succeeding – on quality, handicraft, innovation, reputation and, once again, place.

Brian de Staic Jewellers

What is it about Corca Dhuibhne that seems to attract and inspire so many world-class craftspeople? Another celebrated craft enterprise, this one based in Dingle itself, was founded by jeweller Brian de Staic. De Staic's journey began after he completed his apprenticeship in jewellery making at the College of Art in Cork and spent several years working for a jeweller in Toronto, Canada. While working there, two important insights came to him. First, he realised that he couldn't speak Irish, and though he hadn't cared much about the language before, he now wanted to learn it. Second, he came across an old book of designs from the *Book of Kells*. He marvelled at the intricacy, ornamentation and supreme examples of craftsmanship in these works of art. It was, in his own words, 'the work of angels'.[5] And so, an idea was born. De Staic returned to Ireland and, after someone told him 'if you want to speak Irish properly, live in a Gaeltacht,' he settled with wife Máiréad in Dingle in 1977. Although at first he was a 'one man band', by 1981 he and Máiréad had opened their first shop and workshop.

The Celtic world was a complex one, with a complicated way of looking at life. Celtic artistic designs were no less complicated and expressive. These deep and intricate designs have inspired the art and craft of de Staic. Indeed, the links between culture, history, language, landscape, design and business are vividly drawn in his work, leaving room for imagination and innovation to roam. De Staic's work is focused upon creating jewellery inspired by age-old Celtic traditions in silver and gold, with high-quality, distinctive pieces. All are handcrafted, based upon traditions and motifs inspired by Ogham (the alphabet of Old Irish), the *Book of Kells*, and other Christian and pre-Christian Celtic designs.

> **"** I am intrigued by the opportunity to design using the most inspiring landscape and the wonderful tradition of the Celtic world. Irish metalwork was a centre of excellence in the Celtic world ... I think we lost our way. We took ourselves too seriously. We didn't think about who we are. We should be proud about what we actually created in this country ... If you love something, it will flourish!
>
> *Brian de Staic, 2011*[6] **"**

Brian de Staic Jewellers was commissioned to make personalised jewellery from its Ogham collection as gifts for former US President Bill Clinton, his wife Hillary, and the late actor Paul Newman, among many others. In 2004 the business expanded to America with a shop in California, and in 2005 Máiréad presented the Brian de Staic Jewellery Collection live on QVC, the huge US shopping channel. Ireland's recent economic travails have hurt de Staic no less than many other Irish businesses. Yet, the business remains a successful manufacturing and wholesale company based in its premises on the shores of Dingle Bay, with five retail shops in Ireland and a total of twenty-six people employed. In our view, this enterprise has survived because it realises that Irishness is a recognisable design currency both at home and abroad, it displays a keen awareness of the past, and it offers high-quality jewellery that remains true to a traditional craft.

Wild Goose Studio

Steve Jobs was not the only entrepreneur to have gotten his start in a garage! Here's an Irish version: Wild Goose Studio, an award-winning producer of handcrafted gifts and souvenirs, based in Kinsale, County Cork. It was set up in the late

1960s when two friends, Brian Scott-McCarthy and Kathleen Smyth, pooled their skills to start a venture which later became the Wild Goose Studio. Both had other careers which they continued while they carried out early experimental work to perfect their bronze-casting process, literally in a garden shed. As a result of this collaboration, they bought an old coach house in Kinsale in 1970 with the idea of reproducing ancient Irish artefacts and carvings from Ireland's legacy of High Crosses and making them into attractive souvenirs. To achieve this, they chose to work with a metal cold-casting method, giving the finished pieces a surface of pure bronze or iron, which is a faster and less expensive method than traditional foundry casting.

In the early days, Brian and Kathleen were painstaking in their attention to detail, attempting to reproduce ancient works very precisely. Once complete, they labelled them with simple, factual content, as if they were museum pieces. The pieces were then sold in craft shops around the country and at Shannon Airport. However, Brian had trained as a Jungian psychotherapist and, as a result, developed a keen interest in mythology and symbolism. He began to apply this learning to his work at the Wild Goose Studio, which led to a considerable change both in the type of products being produced and the overall direction of the company.

For instance, Brian started interpreting Ogham symbols or carvings on ancient stone monuments. Ogham, an Early Medieval alphabet, is sometimes called the Celtic Tree Alphabet because it is based on a tradition of ascribing the names of trees to individual characters or letters. Scholars believe most of the surviving inscriptions consist of personal names or marks indicating land ownership, but the meanings have been lost in the mists of time. Thus, Brian began interpreting these carvings himself and putting his interpretations on the labels of the company's products.[7] In this way a nine-hundred-year-old carving on a stone in County Donegal became 'the Celtic Cross of Journeys and Meetings'. This gave the piece a richer story with greater resonance and relevance to customers. By adding meaning to a piece, an emotional connection is created, which makes a customer more likely to buy it. Wild Goose believes that, while customers may be attracted by the imagery of an Ogham inscription as originally intended, in the final analysis, the title and message ascribed to a piece or souvenir is often the reason they make the purchase. By a lucky coincidence of ancient carvings and Jungian psychotherapy, Wild Goose differentiated itself from all other souvenir companies in Ireland.

Brian stepped back from the day-to-day management of the business in 1999, but he continued to dream up ideas for new pieces, working closely with Kathleen to realise these ideas right up until his death in 2004. Brian's son-in-law, Jamie McCarthy-Fisher, joined the company in 1998, becoming Managing Director in 2003. By drawing on mythology, symbols, stories, images and poetry, the Wild Goose Studio believes it taps into the richness of the shared memory that inspires the imagination. Such creations, whilst drawing primarily on the resources of Ireland for inspiration, remain open and accessible to a far wider audience. The Studio's 'cultural giftware' is now sold throughout Ireland and around the world, and has found particular success in catering to tourists. The combination of business, art, spirituality and craft evident in the Wild Goose Studio demonstrate that commerce and spirituality are not opposites, and that success in the one does not necessarily make for failure in the other.

Authentic Clothing

As we saw with Inis Meáin in Chapter 1, the clothing industry provides some striking instances of companies that have developed distinctive niches founded on nostalgia, authenticity and place. Irish linen, for instance, is a product and brand steeped in centuries of tradition, knowledge and skill. In a world of mass production, it stands out as a beacon of authenticity. The craftsmanship of Irish linen has developed over generations, yet the few companies that continue to weave in Ireland cannot compete on price with low-cost global competitors; instead they must concentrate on the high-quality, luxury end of the market.

In Donegal there is also a long tradition of home-spinning yarn, weaving and knitting. What is distinctive about Donegal tweed is its colour, quality, design and provenance; it 'fits' the place from whence it comes and smacks of authenticity, the colours of the yarn being influenced by the beauty of the local landscape. It is very much a premium product and, recently, top fashion designers like Donna Karan, Armani, Ralph Lauren and Hugo Boss have featured the fabric in their collections, lending a fashionable patina to old-fashioned Donegal tweed and bringing it to a wider, globalised audience.[8]

The tradition of hand-woven tweed lives on today, with a small number of weavers working from their own homes. Yet, remarkably, unlike Harris Tweed in the UK, tweed produced anywhere in the world can be labelled Donegal tweed. This is sadly also true for the equally-famed 'Aran sweater', though linen at least *must* be woven in Ireland to bear the Irish Linen Guild's mark of authenticity.

Molloy & Sons in Ardara, County Donegal is one of only a handful of companies which creates authentic Donegal tweed. Father-and-son team Shaun and Kieran Molloy are building on a rich heritage spanning five generations. Like many of the enterprises profiled in this book, inspiration surrounds them, from the dramatic beauty of the ocean, to the sky, hills and mountains, elements echoed in the intricate beauty of the colours and tones found in their tweeds.

❙❙ [Our work represents] the history of the past, the ambition of the future, and the ever-present beauty of the Atlantic coast of Donegal.

Molloy & Sons website, 2012[9] **❙❙**

Another textile business which has been owned by the same family for generations, Cushendale Woollen Mills, has been located on the millrace of the River Duiske in the village of Graiguenamanagh, County Kilkenny since 1880. With textiles, colour is often the first thing buyers look for, and the inspirational mix of local landscape, weather and environment on the colour of Irish textiles offers a distinctive quality which customers value and demand if they buy something from a particular place in Ireland. Philip Cushen, the latest family member to run Cushendale, echoes Louis Mulcahy in suggesting that the colours of the company's fabrics are influenced by the surrounding landscape; evening light changes the local Blackstairs Mountains into a kind of heather colour which the company puts into its textiles.[10] Cushen says that customers want to know the provenance of everything nowadays, which means that skills, craft, heritage and the location of production are unique selling points. One French retailer prominently displays the word *authentiques* when selling Cushendale woollens. In Cushen's own words: 'If they buy something from Ireland, they want something authentic.'[11]

Conclusion

Our purpose in relaying these stories about Irishness, distinctiveness and place is not to hawk cultural commodities. These stories are about confidence, excellence and quality, about standards, not standardisation. We do empathise with the sentiments expressed by London-based artist Brian Kennedy, who has curated several exhibitions for the Crafts Council of Ireland, such as *Forty Shades of Green* in 2005 and *Ecology, Mythology and Technology* in 2007:

❝ One of the biggest problems is that people still play the Irish card, maybe through lack of confidence. The reality is that the work should be seen as European. The people

and galleries I am dealing with don't have any particular interest in Ireland; it is the quality of the work that is paramount. U2 don't sell records because they are Irish; it's because they are a brilliant band.

Brian Kennedy, artist, 2011[12] **"**

Agreed, but while this may be true in pop music, the best policy for a small country is to nurture pride in its distinctiveness which inspires world-class work to help satisfy universal needs. The stories in the next chapter show why this is especially so for firms in the food sector.

7

The Green Island – Farming and Food

It's only a few years since [former Tánaiste] Mary Coughlan was saying that financial services were the way forward and that farming was a sunset industry ... In 2008, when agriculture leaders were flying to Brussels for the final stage of the World Trade Organisation talks, they were even being told on the plane that agriculture was to be put aside: 'You're only meant to be caretakers out there; just keep it looking nice.'
Irish farmer, speaking to the *Irish Times*, 2011[1]

Introduction

How times have changed! Ireland's food sector, its largest industry, is no longer treated as a backwater redolent of the 'bad old days' of frugal self-sufficiency and economic malaise, an ill-developed industry symptomatic of a backward-looking society. Instead, it is loudly affirmed to be a driver of Ireland's recovery and foundation of the newly rediscovered 'real economy'. Agriculture, writ large, undergirds the food sector and continues to play an important role in the Irish economy. It represents 8 per cent of Ireland's GDP and some one hundred and sixty thousand jobs. The domestic economy benefits more than many others from this industry since profits are not repatriated, more of its inputs are purchased in Ireland, and it is more job-intensive than high-tech sectors dominated by foreign multinationals.

Kerrygold

Perceived authenticity is at the core of the most successful international brand-building effort in Irish business history: Kerrygold butter. Although the story is well-known to many, it is still instructive. With the creation of An Bord Bainne (now the Irish Dairy Board) in 1957, Ireland made one of its first forays into enacting the export-driven policies of Seán Lemass and T.K. Whitaker. The thinking was that Ireland's dairy sector, with all of its natural advantages, should be outward looking and internationally competitive. It previously had been, but the advantages were squandered.

Though it ultimately died out, the Cork Butter Exchange was an unrivalled success in international butter trade in the late nineteenth century when Ireland was Britain's largest individual supplier of butter.[2] World prices were even set in Cork. Eventually, however, the butter, sold in bulk and at low prices to middlemen in the UK who blended it to make their own branded products, lost out to branded suppliers from Denmark and New Zealand. The Irish dairy sector developed a less than stellar reputation, and its once formidable share of England's butter market collapsed.

By the late 1950s Ireland was only a minor player in the UK dairy market. Moreover, Ireland's many dairy co-operatives were small and inefficient, with internal squabbling endemic. As the then Chairman of An Bord Bainne warned its first Managing Director, young Tony O'Reilly: 'let me tell you one thing about the Irish cooperative movement and that is there will be very little cooperation!'[3]

The key challenge confronting O'Reilly was to brand Irish butter in a way that made it distinctive and representative of core attributes seen as quintessentially Irish. This is why the Kerrygold label was created in 1962 as a marketing brand for Irish dairy products. It was an inspired choice, since the word 'Kerry' resonated well given the county's tourist attractions, such as the Ring of Kerry and the Lakes of Killarney, and the word 'gold' suggested authenticity and quality.[4] 'Irish

Creamery Butter' was marketed in small consumer packets as 'pure village churned', utterly natural and fresh, conjuring up notions of the village creamery with lines of farmers in donkey carts carrying their milk cans. Similarly, images of contented cows grazing on lush Irish grass were not to be found wanting.

The Irish landscape played a major role in advertising Kerrygold. The company connected its product with the rural landscape, suggesting that by tasting Kerrygold butter, the customer could 'vicariously experience the landscape of Ireland'.[5] One of the best remembered slogans from the time, found everywhere from the sides of lorries to media advertising, was 'Taste Kerrygold – Experience Ireland'. Ireland itself was packaged in a pat of butter!

It was all a great success. Now one of the most recognisable Irish brands worldwide (perhaps first after Guinness, and maybe U2 and *Riverdance*), Kerrygold hints at the natural, good and quality milk that only Ireland can produce. It is Germany's top branded butter with a 14 per cent share of the market there, more than twice as popular as its nearest rival. Of course, the butter has to be consistently high in quality to be sold at a premium price, so Kerrygold is cracking the answer to this intriguing question: if a German can buy domestic butter for less than a euro, why should he or she spend €1.69 on an Irish product?[6] Kerrygold manages to succeed against its rivals by pumping millions into advertising campaigns that are as much about Ireland as butter, creating positive connotations of distinctiveness and purity that largely influence the German image of Ireland, whether true or not.

Small Food Ventures

Though Kerrygold demonstrates a successful approach to food marketing in global markets, most Irish food enterprises are small (72 per cent have less than fifty employees, while 26 per cent have less than ten employees). Ireland is full of stories of entrepreneurial food companies, too numerous to mention. Some are explicitly 'green' or 'organic'. Others operate in more prosaic market spaces. But surely, given the quality of its produce, Ireland can hold its own in the food industry? Not often enough, we're afraid. This is due primarily to the lack of a distinctive sense of place that strongly appeals to universal values. Without this, it is very difficult for Irish food companies to differentiate themselves from competitors. Thankfully, there are notable exceptions, as we describe in the two stories that follow.

Country Choice

Country Choice, an artisan food business based in Nenagh, County Tipperary, was set up in the 1980s by Meath native Peter Ward and his wife, Mary. The company illustrates how a new, indigenous Irish food culture is being born. Internationally-acclaimed US food and travel writer Colman Andrews was so impressed with Country Choice that he wrote a cover story on its work for *Saveur*, the prestigious food magazine.[7] Andrews, an expert on Catalan and Italian cuisine, as well as that from the Riviera, first met Ward in 2002 when he participated in a specialty foods symposium. Listening to the 'drone of officialdom', Andrews was about to flee to the bar when the tenor of proceedings changed: Ward had taken to the podium and, with evangelistic fire, started going on about the glories of farmhouse butter, homemade brown bread and creamy Irish milk.

|| When people come to Ireland wanting to taste Irish food and we serve them something from a German-owned supermarket, that ought to be considered an act of treason.

Peter Ward, 2007[8] **||**

Ward's grandfather owned a grocer's shop and he himself was reared on a traditional family farm. In 1979, while working for a supermarket chain, Ward was sent to Nenagh, where he met Mary D'Arcy, who later became his wife. He recalls: 'I could see that the supermarket business wasn't compatible with our family's philosophy of food. I knew that there was a lot, lot better food in Ireland than was being sold in the supermarkets. I said to myself, "I'm going to sell food – the kind I enjoy," and I thought that Nenagh was the place to do it.'[9] Ward returned to Nenagh in 1982, wed Mary, and the couple opened Country Choice a few years later. They were bucking a trend, Peter remembers: 'Traditional small groceries were closing all over Ireland ... They didn't have the resilience to deal with the onslaught of the chains.'[10]

No surprise that Ward, an enthusiastic Irish speaker, helped found the local Gaelscoil, which teaches through the medium of Irish. Signs in Irish in Country Choice say '*Bia breá blasta*' (Fine-tasting food) and '*Gnó trí Ghaeilge? Bainimis triail as*' (Business through Irish? Let's give it a try).

Country Choice was the inspiration for a sumptuous cookbook which Colman Andrews wrote on traditional Irish cooking. The book, with over two hundred and twenty-five recipes and one hundred evocative photographs, is interspersed throughout with historical and literary references from writers, poets, mythology, legend and old Irish proverbs, like the little gem: '*nua gacha bid agus sean gacha dighe* (every food fresh and every drink mature).[11] TV chef Darina Allen notes in her foreword to the book that Andrews, with his global perspective and vast knowledge of food cultures, recognises how tradition and modernity combine to form a progressive way forward.[12] Calling Ireland 'one of the most exciting food stories in the world today', Andrews warns the Irish to have faith in their distinctiveness and traditions:

❝ [Americans] don't want to go to Dublin and eat in the fifth-best French restaurant they've ever eaten in. It might be an incredible meal, but that's not why they go. They want something they can't get in Paris or New York, whether it's dishes or just the quality of the salmon, or the taste of the grass-fed beef. That's what they'll take home with them. And that's what's going to build the Irish food scene.

Colman Andrews, 2007[13] **❞**

Andrews suggests that no other nation in Western Europe, even Italy or Spain, remains as intimately and pervasively connected to the soil as does Ireland. Though hardly recognised by the average citizen, such a close connection is one of the country's great cultural strengths. Leveraging this rich tradition will yield opportunities that are not only culturally compatible and fully in keeping with Ireland's finest aspirations, but both economically and environmentally sustainable, and consummately on message for Brand Ireland.

Folláin

The potency of 'all natural and Irish made' is also formidably illustrated by Folláin (Irish for 'wholesome'), based in the small County Cork Gaeltacht town of Baile Bhúirne. It is an enterprise that demonstrates the essence of place-based authenticity, character and integrity. Tracing its origins to nearby Cúil Aodha, home of late musician Seán Ó Riada, Folláin produces a range of traditional fresh-fruit preserves, marmalades, jams, relishes, salsas and chutneys. Using 100 per cent natural ingredients and avoiding artificial flavourings, additives and preservatives, the company's first products were based on one-hundred-year-old family recipes. This home-made quality has been retained in its products.

Since its creation in 1983 by Eithne Uí Shiadhail and Máirín Uí Lionaird, the artisan jam-maker has grown from a small cottage industry to one which employs fifteen staff, with sales expected to double to €8 million within three years.[14] Now the biggest jam producer in Ireland, Folláin serves all the major retail grocery chains. The wholesomeness of its preserves and its West Cork provenance are the secrets to its success. It sources much of its fruit locally, and actively encourages local fruit growers. In fact, most of the gooseberries the company uses are sourced from people who merely have a few gooseberry bushes in their garden. Folláin avoids deep discounting, extensive advertising and similar consumer promotions. That is, except for one promotion that co-owner Peadar Ó Lionaird is happy to push: customers who purchase four pots of Folláin preserves can send in 'tokens' from the label and receive in return, not a coupon for more, but a tree to plant. 'I love all trees', says Ó Lionaird, and 'for most people there's no big cost to planting trees and isn't it a wonderful thing to do?'[15]

Origin Green

" Being green and natural is how we have always presented ourselves to the world, and it's how the world has always seen us.

Aidan Cotter, chief executive, Bord Bia, 2012[16] *"*

We maintain that a real challenge facing Irish food producers is less about marketing and more about delivering on their promises: if the image they present through their marketing is one of distinctiveness, purity and naturalness, then the product must live up to this. Perhaps this is self-evident and hardly worth noting, but taking it seriously *would* have huge implications for Irish public policy. It would mean, in fact as well as in theory, pursuing a sustainable agenda and taking active steps to protect and steward Ireland's natural capital.

With its wholesome green image and natural advantages, Ireland is ideally positioned to take advantage of world sustainable food trends, such as the slow food movement. But its global potential in food exports is not simply a matter of supplying commodity products to passive consumers half a world away. Today's consumers want assurance as to food quality and safety. Simply put, they want to know who grew their food, and what practices they used to do it. Bord Bia (the Irish Food Board) does excellent work in this regard, clearly recognising this growing trend and trading heavily on Ireland's natural and agricultural heritage, working to position the country as a high-quality source of 'green' food. Its recent initiatives include the 'Origin Green' sustainability development programme which builds on a foundation of farm-based quality and sustainability audits.

One sector being targeted by the Origin Green initiative is Germany's twelve million so-called 'LOHAS', an acronym for 'Lifestyles of Health and Sustainability', referring to individuals who prioritise a lifestyle of health and sustainable living and are interested in ecologically-correct production in traditional food sectors. Ireland is viewed very credibly by these people as a green island with a mild, moist climate, clean air, untainted soil and abundant grassland. This creates a distinct advantage – an Irish edge – and differentiates Ireland from competitor countries in the minds of consumers who are increasingly concerned about food security in the face of climate change and other environmental challenges.

// People are hungry for authentic products; they're always looking for something new, for a story.
Liam MacHale, manager, Bord Bia's Dusseldorf office, 2012[17] **//**

Liam MacHale of Bord Bia claims Irish food producers are able to trade as much on the island's green image as on their actual products.[18] We agree, but what's impressive about Origin Green is that it doesn't take Ireland's green image for granted.

Origin Green's evidence-based approach to brand truth positions it in a credible way, since at its heart is a sustainability charter that commits participating companies to engage directly with the challenges of sustainability. They must reduce their energy inputs, minimise their carbon footprint and lessen their impact on the environment. Participating companies submit sustainability plans with clear targets for improvement in areas like emissions, energy, waste, water, biodiversity and social responsibility, among others.[19]

Origin Green lays claim to Ireland's resonating perception as a green island and roots that perception in the reality of green credentials. As Bord Bia seeks to develop global perceptions of Irish food into a cohesive Brand Ireland umbrella which touts the openness and transparency of food production, as well as Ireland's heritage of family farming and sustainability credentials, producers will need to be in a position to defend those claims with facts. The explicit promise made by Brand Ireland is simple: 'we are natural and we can prove it.'[20] But in keeping this promise, proof will be what matters – verified and monitored evidence of truth – and authenticity and integrity will be crucial.

// It is a mistake to make a promise that isn't true.
David Bell and Mary Shelman, professors, Harvard
Business School, 2012[21] **//**

Consumers may not be forgiving if promises turn out to be false. Apart from our concern with integrity, it flies completely in the face of attempts by Bord Bia to develop Ireland's reputation as a green, clean, good-food island when another arm of the state gives the go-ahead to carry out trials on genetically modified (GM) potatoes, as Teagasc (Food and Agricultural Development Authority) recently did. We're at one with the Organic Trust: 'Ireland cannot run with the hare and hunt with the hound when it comes to our reputation as a food exporter.'[22]

Ireland surely has a special claim on the colour green; what other nation is so identified with a colour? And not just any colour, but one that is a marker for a clean and natural physical environment. Ireland's unsullied image as a green and pastoral land produces an enduring halo effect that redounds to the benefit of its most important indigenous industries – agriculture and food. It is an effect that not many countries can hope to replicate, but an advantage few Irish enterprises have taken seriously. Yet, as US marketing guru Rick Barrera warns, Irish meat products, in particular, are likely to be consigned to the commodity end of the market unless a branding strategy is built upon Ireland's reputation as a 'green and unspoilt' island.[23]

❙❙ The word terroir is usually associated with wine-making: the combination of factors, including soil, climate, and environment, that gives a wine its distinctive character. In the case of our restaurant, we use the word in order to describe the way in which our food comes from the specific place that is Galway and the West of Ireland. We hope to reveal the distinct and various foodstuffs that make up our particular landscape, through our farms and the wildlands and shores that surround us.

From the website of the Michelin Star Aniar Restaurant, Galway, 2013[24] *❙❙*

Being 'green' is to be well ensconced in the big tent of the 'environmentally friendly'. It implies that a product is pure, unadulterated, natural, energy efficient and ethically produced. In a world in which consumers are increasingly conscious of the environmental impacts of the products they buy, and the quality of what they consume, Ireland's green legacy is, well, golden, and represents a competitive advantage of no small importance. It meets our test of inimitability, uniqueness and rootedness made explicit in earlier chapters of this book. 'Ireland Inc.' may have gotten all the headlines during the years of the Celtic Tiger, but Ireland's real and enduring brand is its green one. Not that the Irish state has recognised this in any meaningful way by going out of its way to protect the nation's legacy as a clean, green-food island. Little tangible support is available, for instance, to the vast range of creative artisan producers up and down the country who do such hard work promoting the image of Ireland as an organic haven.

Food Authenticity

A veritable obsession nowadays with food and its origins is leading to a competitive edge founded on a strong regional or place-based identity. Yet, many consumers possess only a vague sense of the Irishness of food. Terms like 'Irish', 'traditional' and 'local' are meaningless when anyone can label anything with them. What do symbols like 'Guaranteed Irish' and 'Love Irish Food' actually mean? For a product to be allowed to carry the Guaranteed Irish symbol, only 50 per cent of its production process needs to take place in Ireland (for Love Irish Food it is 80 per cent). The only thing Irish about the brand Siúcra, for instance, is its name (meaning 'sugar'), since the last Irish sugar factory closed in 2006 and most of the sugar now comes from Germany. Some brands use a place name to create an impression of where they come from, yet Dubliner Cheese comes from Cork and Donegal Catch contains salmon that may have been farmed anywhere in Ireland, Scotland or even Chile. And not much Kerrygold butter actually comes from Kerry!

// How many harassed shoppers would be able to tell the difference between smoked Irish salmon and Irish smoked salmon? They look similar but the difference could be thousands of miles. Smoked Irish salmon definitely comes from Ireland, while Irish smoked salmon

could come from anywhere, with just the smoke added closer to home.

Conor Pope, consumer affairs correspondent,
Irish Times, 2011[25] **"**

As with Donegal tweed, it is scandalous that no protection exists for Irish food similar to the Appellation d'Origine Contrôlée (AOC) system that protects wine producers in France, Denominazione di Origine Controllata (DOC) in Italy, the Demoninação de Origem Controlada (DOC) in Portugal, or the Denominación de Origen (DO) in Spain. In these countries, words like 'traditional' and 'local' actually have legal definitions. Wine correspondent Tomás Clancy believes a similar Irish system would allow today's generation to reconnect with the variety, diversity and generosity of their own soils and land.[26] He says many consumers are familiar with Parma ham, the wines of Burgundy and the cheeses of Northern Italy, but do not comprehend the complexity of Meath, Kilkenny or Wexford produce. Yet, a unique taste *does* exist in unprotected Irish products, from Gubbeen Cheese to air-dried Connemara lamb. Clancy argues that having a proper Irish labelling system could boost jobs and open up small-scale development for newly delineated and protected products. It would also encourage and support those who want to grow their businesses internationally, offering them a level playing field.

To date only four Irish brands (Imokilly Regato cheese, Connemara Hill Lamb, Timoleague Brown Pudding and Clare Island salmon) use the 1992 EU labelling system which was inspired by the French AOC system mentioned above.[27] This law protects the names of regional foods, and they are given one of three labels: Protected Designation of Origin (PDO), Protected Geographical Indication (PGI) and Traditional Speciality Guaranteed (TSG). In contrast, the number of brands using this system is over fifty in the UK, over one hundred and eighty in Italy and nearly two hundred and thirty in France.

❝ The soil is something to be respected. The soil mixed with water that soils your shoes is not just mud or dirt, for each cubic centimetre of it contains millions of bacteria, nearly all of them the friend of humanity. Soil is a wonderful mechanism of energy, wealth and life. Those who deal with it ought to know how to avoid the creation of dust bowls or erosion from other causes of impoverishment. One of Ireland's greatest needs is respect for the good earth. This will be achieved when farmers have acquired a more intimate knowledge and even love for the soil.
J. Wesley McKinney and W. Salters Sterling, former staff members, Gurteen Agricultural College, 1972[28] **❞**

Again, the Irish language has a potentially important role to play in differentiating Irish produce. Irish has a strong symbolic meaning for Irish people in general, differentiating them from the Anglophone world and tapping into identity and national pride. The use of Irish in advertising reminds consumers of a brand's authenticity, like Homestead's successful bilingual slogan: '*fiúntas ag teacht chun tí*, bringing value home.' So it's astounding to us that so few companies outside the Gaeltacht use bilingual messages to convey an authentic Irish identity for their food products. Féile Foods of Portlaoise, County Laois, which offers a specialist range of meats, is an exception. It uses Irish on its website in the form of short phrases and bilingual headings, which help promote links between its food and Irishness.[29]

A 2007 study showed that consumers, native and foreign, welcome products with bilingual labels, assume they are manufactured in Ireland and have homemade or artisan attributes. In fact, a significant majority are more inclined to buy products that use such labelling.[30] Representatives of the food industry accept that Irish on a label implies 'home-grown' and 'organic'. If only for purely commercial reasons, the language provides an advantage, especially given the trend towards wholesome 'green' products. But even when no immediate economic benefits are discernible, its presence on a label or website helps convey an image of character and integrity.

Future Promise

Average Irish farm incomes more than doubled between 2009 and 2011, while food and drink exports in 2012 reached a record €9 billion.[31] There are continued expectations of robust demand and high prices for Ireland's agricultural products. With world demand for food soaring, prospects for the future seem excellent. Nevertheless, EU subsidies account for 70 per cent of Irish farmers' incomes, while milk quotas are due to be abolished in 2015.[32] Such changes offer opportunities, especially in the dairy sector, since Ireland's grass-based feeding system has huge cost advantages over other European milk producers.

Ireland is blessed with abundant natural resources not only for the production of physical products like infant foods and functional foods (those with health-promoting benefits over and above their usual nutritional value), but also services such as recreation and tourism. There is increasing recognition of the recreational and public value of natural resources like parks and woodlands. Such resources are becoming more appreciated because of their intrinsic value in areas such as natural beauty, biodiversity and water quality.[33]

Natural resources will increasingly provide Ireland's energy and fibre needs, with many of the products derived from fossil fuels likely to be provided by Ireland's plentiful and renewable bio-resources. Bio-energy, for example, has the potential to meet a sizeable proportion of Ireland's future energy needs and create thousands of jobs.

A key challenge is to motivate Ireland's next generation to become innovators in those areas of the bio-economy with great potential, such as high-value, natural, resource-based products and services. This will require a growing emphasis on knowledge-intensity. However, as we pointed out in an earlier chapter, it is crucial that in pursuing scientific knowledge, this is not done to the detriment of the arts, history, geography and the Irish language, which are essential in generating symbolic knowledge or meaning, vital for developing an innovative, competitive economy.

Delivering on the potential of the Irish food sector begins on the farm itself. With the number of full-time farmers in Ireland projected to drop to as low as ten thousand in coming years,[34] a radical strategy is necessary in order to ensure viability. Farmers need to get more involved in marketing artisan 'clean, green, Irish' food, reflected in the image of the traditional family farm. A fundamental change of attitude is needed to respond to market trends since, as a prominent Silicon Valley venture capitalist pointed out, consumers are nowadays as interested in sophisticated meaningful experiences beautifully delivered with food as much as they are with technology products like the iPhone.[35] This means that the history, culture, landscape, and social and natural capital of a territory are important competitive resources. John Feehan, senior lecturer in UCD's Faculty of Agriculture, puts it well: 'farming of the future will have to be more, not less scientific, but the science must be applied to the land in a more intelligent, holistic, ethical and sustainable way.'[36] He adds: 'If there is to be a new and real heart to living in the countryside, farm people themselves have to become the most ardent advocates of a new philosophy in farming.'[37]

The Ballymaloe Cookery School in Shanagarry, County Cork is one path-breaking initiative that promotes this kind of philosophy, fostering intimate connections between food heritage and place. And like the best traditional farms, it is a family-run business. Originally a restaurant opened by Myrtle Allen in the early 1960s, the Cookery School began life in 1983. Allen's daughter-in-law and founder of the school, Darina, understood the vital connection between farming practice and food preparation. Ballymaloe is located in the middle of a one-hundred-acre organic farm, of which ten acres are devoted to organic market gardens, orchards and greenhouses. This means that students learn to cook using the finest and freshest ingredients. The School's philosophy is that the best food starts with the best ingredients, and that 'good food, good health and good farming practices are an inseparable part of the same process.'[38] The School works ceaselessly to avoid waste, uses seasonal produce and is extremely conscious of the 'food miles' its ingredients must travel.

Conclusion

Increasing public concerns about ecosystem damage, animal welfare, food safety and traceability, means more recognition is being given to the immense costs of severing food from its cultural and environmental moorings.[39] Ireland's image as a food brand that stands for sustainability and quality risks being undermined by recent traces of pig and horse DNA found in Irish beef. Consumers are demanding a shift away from the globalised model with its bias towards large-scale, mono-cultural production towards more localised food systems that promote small-scale, diversified farms and healthier communities. Many studies show that such small-scale, diversified agricultural systems often possess a higher output per unit of land than large-scale monocultures.

In the next chapter, we focus on the ancient craft of whiskey-making, which, with its authentic heritage, trades strongly on its Irishness. Advertisements often paint an emotive picture of traditional Ireland at its best, a place where drinking fine whiskey is enjoyed in a convivial atmosphere in the company of friends.

8

The Independent Spirit of Ireland – Brewing and Distilling

Tim Finnegan rising in the bed,
Saying: Twiddle your whiskey around like blazes,
Be the thunderin' Jaysus, did ye think I'm dead?
Lyrics, 'Finnegan's Wake', nineteenth-century Irish
music-hall ballad[1]

Introduction

In a book about authenticity, heritage and distinctiveness, brewing and distilling, once among the few large-scale Irish manufacturing industries, naturally loom large. One of the country's most famous drinks, Baileys, the world's number-one-selling liqueur, is a marriage of Irish dairy cream, Irish whiskey and cocoa extract. Yet, while now accounting for over half of all spirits exported from Ireland, it was dreamed up only in 1974. Most major drink brands, however, can trace their origins to the eighteenth century. Ireland once had a very vibrant local beer industry, but it largely died out during the twentieth century. While a huge number of local craft or artisan breweries have recently sprung up, multinational beer companies own all major 'Irish' beer brands, such as Guinness, Murphy's, Beamish, Harp and Smithwicks.

The relationship between Guinness and Ireland is especially symbiotic, with images so intertwined they even share the harp as emblem. While its giant multinational owner, Diageo, likes to portray Guinness as being about 'authenticity, ritual, community, folklore and language', only since the mid-1990s has it pushed Guinness porter and stout as a specifically Irish product.[2] In recent years, it even cheekily promoted Arthur's Day as an official US holiday. But according to UCD historian Cormac Ó Gráda, Guinness's owners are masters at appropriating tradition and Irishness. While Diageo markets the pint of plain as being as distinctively Irish as hurling and as ancient as Cúchulainn, for much of its history Guinness was far from the national drink.[3] Only after the Great Famine did it make inroads into rural Ireland, tasting quite different from today's brew, which dates only from 1959. Still, Guinness is regarded worldwide as portraying an Irish 'love affair' with drink.

In spite of the undeniable popularity of Guinness, if we had to choose just one product which is intrinsically based on heritage, authenticity and distinct identity, then surely Irish whiskey possesses all these in buckets. It is absolutely unique. For one thing, unlike Scotch whisky, it is spelled with an 'e'. For another, it must be distilled and aged on the island of Ireland and cannot legally be made anywhere else in the world. It was once a substantial export industry; in fact, in the late nineteenth century Irish whiskey dominated world markets.[4] It had no serious competitors. This is no surprise, since whiskey was perfected by the Celts who even gave it its name: in Irish '*uisce beatha*' means 'water of life', giving rise to the word 'whiskey'. Hence, we devote this section to a great story about a drop of the cratur.

Cooley Distillery

As late as 1779, Ireland boasted some one thousand two hundred whiskey distilleries. But the industry in Ireland suffered during the twentieth century, and by the early 1980s there were only two distilleries operating in Ireland, both part of the monopolistic Irish Distillers Group. Enter Irishman John Teeling, who had a vision, beneficially anchored to a practical plan, to revive and reintroduce some of the great brands of Irish whiskey that had faded away during the years of the industry's decline. He achieved this partly through rediscovering ancient distilling techniques and redeploying them to recreate old Irish whiskies, and by attempting something everyone said couldn't be done.

❝ Whiskey is Irish. It really cannot be made to the same quality anywhere else in the world. It is the Irish climate. Irish water is good, as is the barley, but it is the climate that gives Irish whiskey the unique mellow flavour ... The oak barrels breathe in the gentle climate. Too hot, like the US in summer, and the oak expands, allowing quicker and harsher maturation. Too cold, like Canada and Scotland, and the oak closes up, reducing maturation. A moist climate brushed by temperate winds from the Gulf Stream coming in from the Atlantic Ocean is perfect.

John Teeling, 2010[5] **❞**

Teeling, a former academic and old-school serial entrepreneur, was too cautious to invest in property during Ireland's boom, thereby avoiding the travails of the subsequent bust.[6] Based in the Dublin suburb of Clontarf, he always had a preference for more grounded investments – among these a string of mining companies, including diamond and gold exploration companies in Africa, oil and gas exploration companies around the world, and a joint venture exploring for gold on the Wicklow–Wexford border. But we are more interested in another of his pet projects: the creation of the Cooley Distillery which, until it was sold recently, was the only independent, indigenous distiller of Irish whiskey in the world.

With a doctorate from Harvard Business School, Teeling had the original idea for Cooley Distillery in 1970 while studying in the United States. Actually, it was at the Plough and Stars bar in Boston that Teeling and fellow Irishman Willie McCarter (studying at MIT) sat down to swap ideas. McCarter was at the time considering setting up a whiskey operation in his native Donegal. As it turned out, McCarter did some work on reviving whiskey brands but was ultimately unable to secure a supply. The whiskey idea was held in abeyance until 1987 when Teeling (with co-founder Donal Kinsella) established Cooley Distillery with an investment of IR£106,000. The following year McCarter also came on board.

The distillery, originally an alcohol plant that used potatoes to make ethanol, is located on the Cooley Peninsula in County Louth, the site of the ancient and quintessentially Irish epic the *Táin Bó Cúailnge* (*The Cattle Raid of Cooley*). In more recent years, Cooley had also purchased the old Locke's Distillery in Kilbeggan, County Westmeath, which had been empty and unused since its closure in the 1950s. However, members of the local community, including current distillery manager Brian Quinn and his wife Bernadette, came together to preserve the original machinery. Kilbeggan is the oldest licenced whiskey distillery in the world, having operated since well before 1830 (the date of the existing and still functioning pot still).

> **❝** In a period of global economic uncertainty and domestic economic gloom it is a pleasant task to write about an Irish-owned internationally competitive manufacturer. There are few of us around.
>
> John Teeling, 2010[7] **❞**

Today, Cooley employs more than one hundred staff in its distilleries in Kilbeggan and on Cooley Peninsula. It has won numerous awards in its product categories and is now seeking to expand its reach throughout the world in order to reclaim markets lost to blended Scotch whisky and other beverages. But Teeling also had to endure bitter disappointments and setbacks. In 1994, for instance, Ireland's Competition Authority blocked a bid for Cooley by the Irish Distillers Group. On more than one occasion during its first quarter century, Cooley had been on the brink of bankruptcy.

However, sales of Irish whiskey globally have soared in recent years, especially in the United States where it is becoming increasingly popular with younger, more discriminating drinkers. In 2011, Irish whiskey sales in the US grew by 24 per cent, with global sales surpassing five million cases and Cooley enjoying a bumper year of 60 per cent growth.[8] Yet, in a business dominated by giant multinationals, Cooley is a minnow which depends for its survival on the quality of its products, its people and its place.

Until late 2011, this was, in many ways, a David and Goliath story, one in which Cooley played David, the sole independent, Irish-owned producer of Irish whiskey. It was a niche producer that had won every quality award going, including European Distiller of the Year for three years in a row, and World Distiller of the Year in 2009, competing toe-to-toe against the two largest spirits companies in the world. However, in January 2012, the world's fourth-largest drinks company, US-based Beam Inc. (famous for bourbon), completed its purchase of Cooley Distillery in a deal worth around €71 million. The decision to sell was not an easy one for Teeling:

❝ [Selling Cooley is] like walking your only daughter down the aisle and giving her to another man.

John Teeling, 2011[9] **❞**

Despite Beam's purchase, Cooley remains rooted in its Irish location, with current staff and management continuing in place. Matt Shattock, president and CEO of Beam, says: 'We look forward to combining our whiskey expertise, brand-building firepower and strong routes to market with the experience, talent and passion of the Teeling family and the Cooley team to help take these award-winning brands to the next level.'[10]

Teeling told us that Cooley simply had not the firepower to grow to its full potential as an independent player in an oligopolistic and rapidly consolidating (and rapidly growing) global Irish whiskey category. So he and the Cooley board made the difficult decision to sell. Not one to mince words, he says: 'The nerds say we have sold out, and they are right. But it was impossible to compete with the big guys. Now we can get on every shelf in the US market.' He explains:

> *Beam can do in 10 years what it would take Cooley, on its own, 30 years to do. The market opportunity for Irish whiskey is now, and it is substantial. Beam has particular strengths in the main fast-growing Irish whiskey markets and so will be well able to take advantage of this Irish renaissance. It is a bittersweet moment for myself and the other founders as we cede control but, having rebuffed many suitors, we were happy that Beam, which is a pre-eminent whiskey company, will build on the strong foundations laid down over 24 years.*
>
> *John Teeling, 2012*[11]

Yes, some might view this as a defeat, but such a view does not hold up to scrutiny. Cooley is a profitable enterprise with an honourable and inspiring past and a most promising future, even if it is now part of an American multinational. This does not change the fact of its entrepreneurial founding, or of its international reputation for innovation and quality. Cooley is a thriving business created through imagination and determination to succeed, coupled with traditional craft, rootedness and a rich product heritage. It represents both a traditional and a forward-looking, cosmopolitan approach to global markets. As a world-class enterprise, anchored in a rich native tradition and identified with Ireland, yet utterly modern and international, Cooley provides an exemplary model of an innovative enterprise rooted in place. If Beam's purchase of Cooley is successful, and the Cooley brands finally find a place on the shelves of the most lucrative and rapidly growing markets in the world, there will be more production, more employment, and no chance of those activities being outsourced. After all, as Teeling himself says, 'You can only produce Irish whiskey in Ireland.'[12]

The Future of Irish Whiskey

With the sale of Cooley to Beam, all four Irish whiskey makers are now foreign-owned, with the world's leading Irish whiskey brand, Jameson, owned by Pernod Ricard of France (along with Paddy, Powers and others), Bushmills owned by UK-based Diageo, and Tullamore Dew, the world's second-largest Irish whiskey brand, in the hands of William Grant & Sons of Scotland.

Nevertheless, the outlook for Irish whiskey is very positive. In early 2012, Pernod Ricard announced that it would spend €100 million expanding its distillery in Middleton, County Cork and another €100 million on a new maturation facility in nearby Dungourney. Irish whiskey sales are growing faster than any other spirits category globally and are predicted to double in the next five years. Jameson is now in the top thirty of the world's best-selling drinks brands. For the first six months of 2012, and for the first time since the 1930s, Irish whiskey outsold single malt Scotch in the US market. Celebrities are helping out too: sales spiralled after pop icon Lady Gaga described Jameson as 'my long-time boyfriend'.[13]

Ironically, Cooley's purchase by a multinational may also have beneficial knock-on effects for the prospects of small, entrepreneurial distilling ventures, as independents are now likely to start up. This is because, as major players like Beam continue to work their marketing magic and cultivate worldwide demand for Irish whiskey, customers are becoming more educated and sophisticated, and are actively searching for unique, distinctive Irish whiskies with their own taste characteristics. This is having the beneficial effect of fostering the rise of independent boutique distilleries, with new enterprises in Dingle, Belfast and West Cork already operating, and more in the pipeline.

Conclusion

In this and the previous chapter we made a case for authenticity and place as crucial, if often overlooked, sources of competitive advantage for Irish enterprises in the food and drink sectors. Intimately connected with authenticity, place and culture is the even bigger idea of sustainability. This represents a fundamentally different way of envisioning human progress, shifting human values and societal rules away from an emphasis on economic efficiency at all costs towards ecological integrity and social equity. Sustainability implies a change in thinking from individual rights to collective responsibilities, independence to interdependence, luxuries to necessities, short-term to long-term thinking, and growth that benefits a few to development and vitality that benefit all. In other words, sustainability shifts the focus from income to well-being and quantity to quality, implying movement from a linear to a systemic way of thinking. With sustainability now an unstoppable trend, we look in the following chapter at a range of Irish companies, large and small, that illustrate this in practice.

9

Sustainable but Scalable – Global and Green

*To seek out and watch and love Nature, in its tiniest phenomena
as in its grandest, was given to no people so early and so fully
as to the Celt.*
Kuno Meyer, German-born Celtic scholar, 1913[1]

Introduction

Sustainability takes place in a lived world where humankind
and the biophysical earth interact in a welter of experiences,
decisions, meaning and scientific reality.[2] People and business enterprises experience their world in specific places,
yet often the discourse on sustainability is very abstract.
Throughout this book we maintain that Ireland's place-
based enterprises, whose resources, productive activities
and ownership are anchored in specific local places, possess
an authentic sense of place, or an Irish edge. Feeling at home
in a specific place, such enterprises are more likely than
conventional ones to act with integrity in pursuing locally
sustainable and beneficial outcomes.

Ireland, blessed with an abundance of renewable
resources and the intellectual and human capital to harness
them, is well positioned to play a leading role in a sustainable, twenty-first century global economy. This is suggested
by the country's heritage of early nature poetry which, with
its distinct love of place and lamentation of exile from a

cherished territory, occupies a unique position in literature. It is very unfortunate that this inheritance is largely forgotten. Yet, with this imaginative tradition, Ireland has a great opportunity to position itself in the vanguard of the sustainable innovation movement, where emotions are a powerful driving force. However, so far, despite the country's many natural advantages, Ireland clearly has been a laggard in this regard: its past and present performance in preserving the natural environment has been less than stellar. But all is not lost. Fortunately, even in the depths of recession, there are competitive, world-class Irish enterprises that are taking a sustainable approach – enterprises that utilise natural renewable resources in Ireland to compete internationally.

While the 'greenness' of these companies is different from those that overtly trade on their 'Irishness', they go well beyond merely flying the green flag. They offer something deeper and even integral to both the preservation of Ireland's natural environment and the development of native enterprises that can compete, and win, in intensely competitive global markets. They play the green card well and are critical components of a sustainable economic system, recognising their stewardship responsibilities to the natural environment that sustains them, the society in which they are embedded, and the distinctive culture that shaped them. This is not to suggest that such firms will overthrow the primacy of multinational investment, but they do provide much-needed balance.

Global Enterprises

Some enterprises like Coillte and Bord na Móna are state-owned and, though fully commercial, their remit is to balance market and non-market goals. While Ireland has one of the lowest percentages of forest coverage in the world, Coillte, the country's largest landowner, is charged with managing its forest estates (which make up 7 per cent of the land cover) sustainably. Coillte obtained Forest Stewardship Council (FSC) certification in 1992, instrumental in growing its exports to the UK. So it is surprising that the government announced in 2012 it intended selling Coillte's forests. While this proposal was subsequently refined into a sale of the right to harvest Coillte's timber, and now appears to be shelved altogether, it is in seeming disregard of significant recreational, environmental and social considerations. The money received from such a sale would doubtless not take into account such less-quantifiable losses, while the action could also put the agricultural and food industries at risk.

Meanwhile, Bord na Móna, the turf development board which was set up in 1934 to harvest Ireland's peat (or turf) resources, now extends far beyond its original remit. Today, it is retooling its vision and strategy to be consistent with an ethos of sustainable development. Its 'new contract with nature' commitment articulates a vision of becoming socially and environmentally sustainable, with a focus on renewable energy and resource recovery. The company has also vowed not to drain or open any additional bogs or peatlands in the future.[3]

A few Irish businesses are already major international players in sustainability, though established only in recent decades by remarkable entrepreneurs. One enterprise, Glen Dimplex, is the world's largest manufacturer of electrical heating products. Headquarted in Dublin, the Glen Dimplex Group has over ten thousand employees and a value of €2 billion, yet it is still privately held.[4] It is hard to believe the company had only seven employees when it was set up as Glen Electric in 1973 by Martin Naughton and four colleagues in Newry, County Down to manufacture oil-filled radiators. Glen Dimplex today is at the vanguard of a low carbon revolution, with innovative systems that enable customers around the world to reduce their CO_2 emissions. Another exemplary firm is the County Cavan based global provider of sustainable building products, Kingspan, founded as a small engineering company in the 1960s by

Eugene Murtagh. With 2012 revenues of over €1.6 billion,[5] Kingspan is at the forefront of green design and construction around the world.

Both Glen Dimplex and Kingspan might be classified as sustainable global enterprises, in that while being highly mobile multinational organisations they also recognise the importance of the local and the imperative to co-create social and economic value in all locations in which they operate.[6] While they are not place-based in the sense we use throughout this book, they are place *sensitive*, in that they possess a more dispersed and diffused sense of place than that of place-based enterprises. For instance, Glen Dimplex, with a logo inspired by Celtic knots and containing the tagline 'thinking globally, acting locally', sees itself as an international rather than a multinational company.[7] While global operations are overseen from its head office in Dublin, the company retains a devolved structure. Individual companies within the group are given substantial autonomy and power to make decisions, and encouraged to be progressive and entrepreneurial while operating with total integrity and transparency. No doubt such values, reflecting those of the company's founder and now executive chairman, Martin Naughton, helped keep Glen Dimplex out of the recent global financial mire.

Kerry Group

Few of Ireland's global business success stories are as compelling as that of the Kerry Group. It is over forty years since production began at a half-completed milk-processing facility in the muddy 'Canon's Field' outside Listowel, County Kerry. If its beginnings as a dairy co-operative were modest, expectations for its success, or even survival, were more modest still. Many had doubted the project would even get off the ground, seeing Kerry as something less than a hotbed of entrepreneurial activity and economic potential.

❝ What does Kerry want a processing plant for? Sure, there's nothing down there but mountains, heather and rushes.

Irish Government official, late 1960s[8] *❞*

But Kerry beat the odds and, decades before the Celtic Tiger roared, it began to weave its own home-grown, rags-to-riches story. The company has grown from a small, woefully-under-capitalised dairy co-operative, producing a limited number of commodity products, to a multinational food ingredients and consumer foods company with more than twenty-four thousand employees in over forty countries, market capitalisation of nearly €7.9 billion, and 2012 revenues of €5.8 billion, with profits before tax of €482 million.[9] Indeed, it is probably the world's pre-eminent specialised food ingredients and flavourings company, and the most technologically advanced. Its customer book is a who's who of blue-chip global food companies, spanning all major food categories.

It is a fool's errand to attempt to boil Kerry's success down to any one attribute; there are a number of key success factors. Enormous credit must go to its former managing director and prime architect of early success, Denis Brosnan, who grew Kerry from a tiny co-operative struggling to survive in a commodity business. Much of its growth is attributable to its aggressive, even audacious, acquisition strategy. It first engaged in targeted acquisitions in Ireland, then the UK and North America, and eventually throughout South America, Asia and Europe. Early on, it developed and demonstrated uncommon skill in combining new acquisitions with its existing businesses and merging them into a cohesive, and global, Kerry brand. While rooted in Ireland, it has always looked outward.

❝ We have got to lift our heads beyond the borders of this small country. It's a big world out there!

Denis Brosnan, 2001[10] *❞*

131

Apart from core technologies and global resources that have put it at the forefront of providers of 'food solutions' to processors and services companies, Kerry's success is also related to the uncommonly sound leadership it has enjoyed. Starting with the visionary Brosnan, to the strategically-minded Hugh Friel, and home-grown current CEO Stan McCarthy, all emphasised the craft of strategic planning and implementation, coupled with a focus on operational discipline at every level. It's an organisation that has always played to win, consistent with the famed 'green and gold' Gaelic football code of its native Kerry. Some have argued (with only a little hyperbole) that these Kerry roots have played a role in the Group's success. While Tralee does not boast a surfeit of corporate headquarters, the Kerry Group remains based there, controlling its expansive global operations from Prince's Street. Although Kerry long ago evolved into a publicly-held company, its original owners, the Kerry farmers who helped found the enterprise, still maintain significant ownership. Through both the shareholding that the Kerry Co-operative Creameries retains in the Kerry Group (17 per cent) and shares owned directly by local farmers and other residents (estimated to be as high as 45 per cent), Kerry Group remains closely connected to the county.

This connection with Kerry and its people is more than merely shareholdings or providing jobs (the company employs around five thousand people in Ireland). The Kerry Group has been vitally engaged in the life of the community and giving back to that community for the past forty years. From sponsoring the Kerry Gaelic football team, a natural fit as it's another high achiever, to funding countless charities throughout the county, there are few good local causes that have not benefitted in some way from the Kerry Group's contributions. An example of this is the company's sponsorship of the Endeavour Programme, run in partnership with a private company (Tweak), a state organisation (Shannon Development) and an academic institution (the Institute of Technology, Tralee), which fosters business start-ups and entrepreneurship.

// Today's founders need to be ready for the opportunities and threats posed by a globalised world ... There is a very strong entrepreneurial spirit in Ireland; it just needs to be unlocked and nurtured.

Stan McCarthy, CEO Kerry Group, 2011[11] //

The Group's success has meant many things to the county itself, not all of them concrete and tangible. There have been psychological benefits, since such success no doubt fosters deep local pride, a spirit of self-reliance, high standards of achievement and an unwillingness to accept defeat or mediocrity. But while it may be difficult to measure their impact on collective confidence, such factors do bestow significant economic favours.

What impresses us about the Kerry Group's success is that it did not stem from a low corporate tax regime or from government incentives or inducements. The fact that it went on to prosper is a testament to the abilities of its employees, the vision of its founders and its leadership team, as well as the faith of its shareholders. It is also a testament to the overarching belief of all those involved in the company that it could compete successfully on a global scale. Crucially, this belief was backed up by hard work and continuous innovation.

Will another Kerry Group emerge in Ireland? Can other enterprises from 'the back of beyond' compete in a savagely competitive global arena, and succeed? The story of the Kerry Group offers an impressively emphatic, positive, and inspirational answer: *is féidir linn!*[12]

Small Green Ventures

In an increasingly globalised world, great opportunities exist for indigenous companies that marry traditional skills and quality, especially if leveraged with online trading. Craft and design, in particular, has a major role to play in helping make connections between environmental sensitivity and the creative process, linking what is real to what makes Ireland unique. Just as surely, Ireland's past poverty could form the springboard for a sustainable innovation economy. The way people attempt to re-use materials or search locally to reduce transport costs today came naturally to people in the past. With a need to heat houses economically becoming increasingly important as energy supplies dwindle, the Irish future may mirror its past. Throughout Ireland's history, householders, who often lived in cramped conditions, ingeniously produced space-saving designs from local renewable materials.[13] No doubt the same approach would be suitable for environmentally sustainable furniture today.

Several small Irish companies show how economic benefits can be generated from such an ethic of sustainability. Bunbury Boards, founded in 2008 in County Carlow, for example, produces a range of distinctive, hand-crafted chopping boards from hardwoods actively managed for sustainability. What makes Bunbury Boards distinctive is that all the wood used to make its products is not only sourced from downed trees in the woodlands on the company's own Lisnavagh Estate, but it is also fully traceable. Each board is individually stamped and coded, and this code enables purchasers to obtain a 'tree report' from the company's website detailing the story of the tree (with photo) from which the board was made and explaining what was done to replace it.

Celtic Roots Studio, based in Ballinahown near Athlone in County Westmeath, uses another of Ireland's distinctive natural resources to create sculptures and gifts – bogwood. The bogwood, dug up as a by-product of harvested midland bogs, is primarily derived from oak and over five thousand years old. While most enterprises can't trace their lineage that far back, a sense of place ought still to be at their core. In today's world, even if an enterprise is less than conscientious about its carbon footprint, its customers increasingly are. This is why consumers often choose, and are willing to pay a premium for, a distinctive and sustainable product or service. As an island nation, Ireland can excel in this regard, and has great potential to prosper in natural resource sectors where it possesses a special advantage. Take seaweed: Ireland is ideally positioned for harvesting this resource, since the island straddles both the northern limit of the geographical range for some warm-water seaweed species and the southern limit for other cold-water species. Seaweed is also a sustainable form of raw material that regenerates over a short period of time. World production of seaweed has increased rapidly in recent years, as demand for its flavour and other functional properties is growing. Nevertheless, Ireland's seaweed output remains miniscule, with most of the production going into high-volume, low-value commodities such as fertilisers and animal feeds rather than low-volume, high-value products such as food, cosmetics and therapies.

VOYA

VOYA is a rare example of an enterprise with high-value-added products that harness the potential of Ireland's extraordinary seaweed resources. Gathering seaweed is ingrained in the traditions of many economically-marginal coastal communities along Ireland's west coast. Indeed, the therapeutic and recuperative qualities of wild seaweed have long been known in Ireland. At the beginning of the twentieth century there were an estimated three hundred seaweed bathhouses in Ireland, mainly along the west coast, but by the end of the twentieth century, only a handful remained.

The small town of Strandhill, County Sligo once contained nine seaweed bathhouses, but these were long gone by 1999 when the story of VOYA begins. At the time, local athlete Neil Walton had risen to become one of the top triathletes in the world, a rise he attributed in part to the recuperative properties of natural seaweed baths. After hearing from fellow athletes about how seaweed baths are used to remove toxins from the body and to accelerate the healing process, Neil was prompted to investigate the tradition of this therapy and the history of seaweed baths in Strandhill. A few years later, Neil's brother Mark, who was working in Dublin for a financial services company, and Mark's wife, Kira, returned to Strandhill and, together, the family revived the town's tradition of seaweed baths by opening Celtic Seaweed Baths, later to become VOYA. Still one of only a few such bathhouses in the country, VOYA entices customers from all over the world. With some forty thousand visitors a year, the bathhouse has become one of Sligo's most popular landmarks.

With the bathhouse's initial success, VOYA looked at setting up another seaweed bath in other locations, but it was at the time when silly money was being thrown at any property in a remotely commercially-zoned area.[14] So the company looked at other opportunities. At the time, Mark was looking at ways to leverage higher revenue spends from the baths' visitors through more premium services and retail sales. He looked for a supplier but couldn't source anything. It was clear that there was considerable demand for organic products that could duplicate something of the seaweed experience for home or spa use, but a search revealed that no certified organic seaweed products existed.

The Waltons knew that conventional cosmetics producers use chemicals which could destroy the beneficial properties of natural seaweed and also damage the environment. This was an unacceptable compromise.[15] After ten years of effort, they eventually succeeded in creating the first genuinely organic seaweed-based cosmetic products in the world, developing and perfecting a complex method of preserving seaweed naturally. The method replicates how seaweed becomes exposed and dries out during the ebbing of spring tides, enabling VOYA to retain the unique qualities and effects of seaweed in its beauty and skincare products.

The Waltons realised low quality 'Oirish' products had limited appeal in the international marketplace so they created the brand VOYA, symbolising the voyage on the sea which their products and seaweed baths represent. While based on the Irish seaweed tradition, the brand is contemporary, luxurious and organic, as well as sustainable.[16] And it's clearly working: the company's turnover has grown by 100 per cent every year since its launch. In addition to sales in Ireland, VOYA exports to over thirty countries, mostly in Europe, the Middle and Far East, and North America. It punches well above its weight in winning high-profile business, supplying a range of upscale international clients, including luxury hotels and spas like the Burj Al Arab and Talise Spa in Dubai, the Waldorf Astoria and The Landmark in London, St. Regis Princeville in Hawaii, and the Four Seasons resort in Azerbaijan, as well as the Queen Mary 2 (shipping company Cunard Line's flagship ocean liner), and even Richard Branson's private yacht! All the company's products contain extracts from organic wild and hand-harvested seaweed, keeping its carbon footprint to a minimum, and VOYA is earning a reputation for sustainable practices and a disciplined approach to maintaining the integrity of its organic certification regime.

Conclusion

With so much attention focused on Ireland's economic troubles, and public policy obsessed with attracting foreign investment and creating a 'smart' economy, it is easy to forget that the central challenge of this century will be to develop ways for nine billion human beings (world population estimated by 2042) to not only survive, but flourish on earth, without destroying life-supporting ecosystems.[17] To accomplish this, we can no longer simply devour the earth's non-renewable resources and deplete its stock of natural capital. Indeed, the parsimonious utilisation and conservation of finite, non-renewable natural resources, and a rebalancing towards the use of renewable resources, must take centre stage.

Although Ireland's air and water quality generally remain good, the Environmental Protection Agency (EPA) projects that while the country's greenhouse gas emissions comply with its Kyoto Protocol obligations (2008–2012), there is a significant risk it will not meet its EU 2020 targets even under the best-case scenario.[18] Its energy intensity (use per unit of GDP) is the worst amongst Organisation for Economic Co-operation and Development (OECD) member countries. Notwithstanding this dismal record, the government's recent 'Action Plan for Jobs 2012' describes leveraging an 'established international image' as the 'Emerald Isle' which can be built upon to promote Ireland's 'green offering'.[19] Regardless of the rhetoric about 'improving the branding of Ireland's image' and capitalising on opportunities, particularly in renewable energy, enterprises that constitute the Irish 'green economy' receive little tangible support. Still, a game-changing low-carbon strategy has huge business potential for firms, both domestically and internationally.[20]

A culture of sustainability is invariably linked to resource productivity and innovativeness. Economic competitiveness, social equity and environmental performance are compatible, if not mutually reinforcing. The new paradigm of competitive advantage rests not on a static model, involving a trade-off between the environment and the economy, but a dynamic one based on innovation. Innovation allows companies to use inputs more productively, thus offsetting the costs of improving environmental impacts. Doing more and better with less, or redesigning products and services that mimic biological behaviour to minimise waste, should be central to Irish economic policy. Although those vested in promoting the orthodox economic order may kick and scream, sustainable development will, of necessity, become the dominant paradigm for the twenty-first century. Indeed, a sustainable economy is the ultimate 'smart' economy.

III

Towards 2016

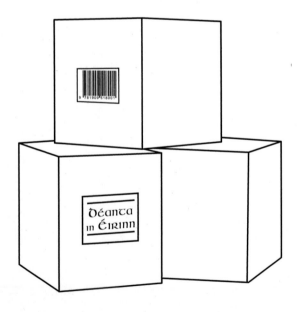

10

An Authentic Republic

The real riches of the Irish nation will be the men and women of the Irish nation, the extent to which they are rich in body and mind and character.

Michael Collins, Irish patriot, 1922[1]

In the run up to the centenary of the Easter Rising in 2016, many questions will be asked, and rightfully so, about the extent to which the contemporary Irish state has met the aspirations outlined for it by its founders. Such soul-searching is healthy – and long overdue. President Michael D. Higgins set the bar high with recent assertions that Ireland suffers a far more serious intellectual and moral crisis than the economic one that so pervades media discussions.[2] A long-time critic of the market model dominated by what he calls 'radical individualism', the President argues that Ireland failed since independence to achieve a real republic.[3] In a speech given in February 2012, he pointed out that by the time of the recent boom, Ireland's leaders and people had all but lost a connection with the cultural and political elements of national revival which might have provided an ethical brake on the excesses of the recent boom.[4] The French philosopher Paul Ricoeur saw that a crucial paradox faced a country like Ireland on the road towards modernisation when it felt the need to jettison its cultural past, the very *raison d'être* of the nation:

❧ Whence the paradox: on the one hand, it [the nation] has to root itself in the soil of its past, forge a national spirit, and unfurl this spiritual and cultural revindication before the colonialist's personality. But in order to take part in modern civilization, it is necessary at the same time to take part in scientific, technical and political rationality, something which very often requires the pure and simple abandon of a whole cultural past.

Paul Ricoeur, French philosopher, 1961[5] **❧**

Nobody understood this paradox described by Paul Riceour better than the architect of the modern Irish economy, former Taoiseach Seán Lemass. Out-of-control sectional interests in the Ireland of the sixties were partly the product of the revolution Lemass had engendered. Yet, he also recognised that the idealism which had driven him and many of his generation was no longer a driving force for the majority of his fellow citizens.[6] He rightly predicted great social changes in Ireland within forty years, with materialism widespread due to growing prosperity. While he welcomed change, he was pessimistic about a future in which the good qualities of the Irish people would be lost; he saw the search for a restored sense of motivation and purpose as paramount.

The danger signs were also apparent around that time to Taoiseach-to-be Garret FitzGerald. He argued that native traditions have a vitally important emotional role to play in development – resources to draw on for inspiration, thought and action.[7] He believed that unless Irish society became proud of its origins, and felt closely linked to its past, it would develop a rootlessness inimical to the establishment of any stable society. FitzGerald held that while Ireland's rich traditions provided a unique wealth of ideas and ideals on which to build a distinctive way of thought, in practice the country had made no effort to construct such an integrated philosophy.

Revitalising such an integrative national spirit was a driving force for this book, but we have no wish for the terms we have used throughout – culture, identity, tradition and place – to be seen as advocating an exclusive, singular approach to contemporary Irish culture. Ireland is, thankfully, now a multicultural society, nourished by the energy and pioneering spirit of the New Irish; deep commitment to the place they now call home will surely lead to creative and vibrant communities.

❦ If we must – as we must – learn truly to esteem and love the cultures of other peoples, and the quality and uniqueness of what they do, surely it can only be from a knowledge and love of what we do ourselves, of its own quality and uniqueness.
Justin Keating, Irish Labour Party politician, 2003[8] **❦**

A grand vision of a successful society, anchored by meaning and practical idealism, comprising people of different cultural backgrounds who share a communal commitment to place, is a unifying project that will drive innovation, transformational learning and sustainable competitiveness. Yet, it is fair to acknowledge that, at present, Ireland is operating in something of an imaginative vacuum, bereft of any overarching vision. Former President Mary Robinson, in a speech at the 2009 commemoration of the death of Michael Collins in the village of Béal na Bláth, County Cork, commented that the absence of 'a vision of ourselves' lies at the heart of Ireland's crisis, suggesting that 'for the country to emerge from a crisis of this magnitude it must have a vision of where it hopes to go and what it sees as its future.'[9] Despite this, she also saw the opportunity, as we ourselves do, for an innovative vision with Ireland becoming a leader in climate justice. To succeed, the country needs to wholeheartedly invest in green jobs, mitigate its greenhouse gas emissions and develop alternative indigenous energy sources.

But leaders must do much more. In a recent opinion piece, Oscar-winning British film director Lord Puttnam argues that a particular type of ethic, attitude or education must be at the core of national renewal. He says that all his reading leads him to the conclusion that what Michael Collins felt worth fighting and dying for was an Ireland that acted as a beacon to the world – a nation culturally and socially better and fairer than its historical oppressor:

> **"** It's now down to a test of will to invest the time, effort and energy to rediscover those things for which Ireland has been celebrated: quality of learning, culture, imagination, inventiveness, a sense of 'community' and 'place' that the world has in the past – and, please God, will once again – come to admire, and possibly seek to emulate.
>
> *Lord Puttnam, British film director, 2011*[10] **"**

To achieve this vision, Michael Collins saw, as did James Connolly, that without intellectual independence, political independence would be a pyrrhic victory. Arthur Griffith, founder of Sinn Féin (meaning 'ourselves'), did not appreciate that economic self-sufficiency could not be achieved without independent thinking. Collins recognised links between the marginalisation of the Irish language and a lack of intellectual thinking by leaders on social and economic issues, and saw the revival of the language as a crucial goal. Speaking shortly before his death of the challenges facing the new state, he said:

> **"** The biggest task will be the restoration of the language. How can we express our most subtle thoughts and finest feelings in a foreign tongue? Irish will scarcely be our language in this generation, or even perhaps in the next. But until we have it again on our tongues and in our minds we are not free …
>
> *Michael Collins, 1922*[11] **"**

Since Collins's time, many intellectuals, such as Seán de Fréine and Breandán Ó Doibhlin, have argued that the underlying values driving revival are essential ingredients for sustainable economic success. It seems likely that similar deficiencies of character and lack of personal responsibility damage civic morality and integrity in business. Yet, contemporary critics of the recent financial collapse seem not to recognise this. A recent piece on moral and economic bankruptcy by prominent historian Diarmuid Ferriter, for instance, failed to address the issue at all.[12]

Strong vision and leadership is essential. The troika of the European Central Bank (ECB), the European Commission (EC) and the International Monetary Fund (IMF) appears to be firmly in the driver's seat of Ireland's economic affairs, and can scarcely be expected to provide an inspirational vision. And even if it could, perhaps the Irish would find such a vision less than ideal for a small island nation whose very sovereignty, at the very least, has been seriously compromised. What would the martyrs of 1916 and, indeed, Collins himself, have to say about that?

In this context, it is useful to ask direct and even painful questions about the Irish economy generally and Irish indigenous enterprises more particularly: to what extent does the economy serve the interests of the nation and its people – economically, socially and environmentally? How able are indigenous Irish enterprises to survive and thrive in an increasingly competitive global arena? Why is the country so dependent on the whims of multinational companies? Why can't we emulate the world-leading but specialised indigenous sectors of small Northern European countries like Finland and Norway? How will Ireland and its people maintain control over their own economic destiny? What is Ireland's place, economically, socially and morally, in the globalised twenty-first century economic system?

A successful society, after all, is more than just a productive economy. The contemporary obsession with acquiring additional foreign direct investment may well be counterproductive, to the extent that it overlooks the innovative and entrepreneurial capacities that exist in this country today. Ireland's competitive position will increasingly be determined by its ability to satisfy international demand through creativity, innovation, meaning, uniqueness, distinctiveness in quality, and excellence in service. A potent approach to improve productivity and innovation is to nurture tacit knowledge, heritage and tradition alongside a new emphasis on sustainability, biodiversity and quality of life. If cultural identity and sense of place are central to Ireland's self-image, it will contribute to wholeness, integrity, civic responsibility, aesthetic sensibility and ecological stewardship. John Feehan, senior lecturer in UCD's Faculty of Agriculture, sounds a warning:

ff We have narrowed our exploration of Irish culture to literature and performance art with enormous success and the blossoming of a new sense of Irish pride. Our official sense of national identity has become reduced to a rearguard defence of the national language. But we have all but lost our geographically particular sense of closeness to the land, an affinity once unique to each rural community, a closeness out of which our oral culture was developed, which nurtured it and made it what it is.
John Feehan, UCD academic, 2003[13] *ff*

Nevertheless, we are encouraged by widespread evidence that in a rapidly-globalising world the local is more important, and more valuable, than ever. The education of Ireland's young is a particular challenge. Here's an intriguing question: what might be the impact on the young, many of whom are suffering from alienation during these difficult economic times, if a concerted effort was made to foster a strong sense of cultural identity? Or, can Ireland's youth be given a sense of empowerment and self-reliance through culture, especially when economically and politically many feel desperately disenfranchised? We are convinced the answer to both questions is 'yes'.

A profound sense of place helps encourage an ethos of high quality and high aspirations, a singular work ethic, and empowered innovative people, communities and enterprises. To face change with confidence, people must feel rooted in their own identity and connected to their natural surroundings. Ultimately, policies that tap into the spirit, emotions and deep-felt nature of a people can provide a powerful and inimitable competitive advantage. Irish enterprises of all sizes, building upon the country's distinct cultural and natural resources, have the capacity to be in the vanguard of the creation of a smart economy and a successful society. For all the doom and gloom in contemporary Ireland, there is really no better time to begin this challenging, but ultimately exhilarating, journey.

Endnotes

Preliminary Matter

1   Plunkett, H. (1904), *Ireland in the New Century*, London: John Murray, p. 291.
2   Heaney, S. (1995), *Seamus Heaney - Nobel Lecture: Crediting Poetry*, available from: <http://www.nobelprize.org/nobel_prizes/literature/laureates/1995/heaney-lecture.html>, accessed 6 May 2013.
3   Horgan, J. (1997), *Seán Lemass: The Enigmatic Patriot*, Dublin: Gill & Macmillan, p. 305.
4   Bradley, F. and Kennelly, J.J. (2008), *Capitalising on Culture, Competing on Difference: Innovation, Learning and a Sense of Place in a Globalising Ireland*, Dublin: Blackhall Publishing.

Chapter 1

1   *Levi's Visit* (2011), Inis Meáin Knitting Co. (video), available from: <http://inismeain.ie/entry/levis_visit>, accessed 2 July 2013.
2   'How to spend it: A chic knitwear outpost in the Aran Islands', *Financial Times*, 4 December 2011.
3   *Ibid.*
4   The company's promotional materials also carry the Irish phrase: '*Go maire tú is go gcaithe tú é*' ('May you live long to wear it').
5   de Blacam, T. (2012), interviewed by Finbarr Bradley, 12 March.
6   'Smart men of Aran', *Agenda Magazine* (*Sunday Business Post*), 8 January 2012.
7   McKenna, J. and McKenna, S. (2008), *The Bridgestone 100 Best Restaurants in Ireland 2009*, Durrus, County Cork: Estragon Press.
8   'Top tables', *Irish Times*, 5 June 2010, and 'Bia blasta', *Irish Times*, 28 June 2008.
9   de Blacam, R. (2011), interviewed by Finbarr Bradley, 9 November.
10 *Ibid.*

11 'The delectable dozen: best restaurants of 2011', *Financial Times*, 2 December 2011.
12 'Fresh and wild', *Financial Times*, 21 October 2011.

Chapter 2

1 Máirtín Ó Direáin (1984), Extract from the poem 'Cranna Foirtil' ('Stout Oars') in *Selected Poems: Tacar Dánta*, Newbridge, County Kildare: The Goldsmith Press, pp. 54–5.
2 Hederman, M.P. (1985), 'Poetry and the Fifth Province', *The Crane Bag*, 9(1), pp. 110–19.
3 Faulkner, W. (1975), *Requiem for a Nun*, New York: Random House, p. 80 (original work published 1951).
4 Indecon International Economic Consultants (2010), 'Economic Significance and Potential of the Crafts Sector in Ireland', Report for the Crafts Council of Ireland, November, available from: <http://www.ccoi.ie/content/view/361/191/>, accessed 21 April 2013.
5 See www.heritagecouncil.ie.
6 Mannix, L. (2010), 'In Appreciation of Painted Signs', *Heritage Outlook*, winter, pp. 24–7.
7 'Our tourism share plummets in spite of record marketing spend', *Irish Independent*, 2 January 2012.
8 'Failed tourism policy is costing money and jobs', *Irish Times*, 3 August 2012.
9 'Brand Ireland must not be allowed to die', *Irish Independent*, 3 January 2010.
10 Fáilte Ireland and Arts Council (2010), *Cultural Tourism Seminar*, 18 November.
11 'French lesson for our arts ministers', *Irish Times*, 27 June 2008.
12 'We must retake economic control now', *Irish Times*, 9 January 2009.
13 Carter, S.L. (1996), *Integrity*, New York: HarperPerennial.
14 'Exploiting our heritage', *Irish Times*, 20 February 2012.
15 'Celebrating St Patrick's Day', *Irish Times*, 17 March 2011.
16 Hock, D. (2005), *One from Many: VISA and the Rise of the Chaordic Organization*, San Francisco, CA: Berrett-Koehler Publishers.
17 Kjaer, A.L. (2006), 'Emotional Consumption', *Copenhagen Institute for Futures Studies*, Future Orientation/2, available from: <http://www.cifs.dk/scripts/artikel.asp?id=1364&lng=2>, accessed 21 April 2013.
18 Pink, D. (2006), *A Whole New Mind: Why Right-Brainers will Rule the World*, New York: Penguin Group.

19 *Ibid.*
20 Castells, M. and Himanen, P. (2002), *The Information Society and the Welfare State: The Finnish Model*, Oxford: Oxford University Press.
21 'How Jobs put passion into products', *New York Times*, 7 October 2011.
22 Rellis, P. quoted in Ryan, J. (2008), *The Next Leap: Competitive Ireland in the Digital Era*, Dublin: Institute of International & European Affairs, p. 7.
23 Mathews, P.J. (2003), *Revival: The Abbey Theatre, Sinn Féin, The Gaelic League and the Co-operative Movement*, Notre Dame: University of Notre Dame Press.
24 Hackett, F. (1941), *I Chose Denmark*, New York: Doubleday, Doran & Company, Inc.
25 'GAA has tapped into growth of sport as substitute for religion', *Irish Times*, 24 August 2009.
26 O'Malley Greenburg, Z. (2011), 'U2, Gaelic Football, and the Price of Fame in Ireland', *Forbes*, 8 August, available from: <http://www.forbes.com/sites/zackomalleygreenburg/2011/08/31/u2-gaelic-football-and-the-price-of-fame-in-ireland/>, accessed 21 April 2013.
27 'On home ground', *Irish Food*, 2007 International Edition, p. 44.
28 'Fitting way to mark a special day', *Irish Examiner*, 2 November 2009.
29 Fanning, J. (2010), *The Mandarin, the Musician and the Mage: T.K. Whitaker, Seán O'Riada, Thomas Kinsella and the Lessons of Ireland's Mid-Twentieth-Century Revival*, Unpublished PhD thesis, UCD, November.
30 Marcus, L. (1981), 'Seán Ó Riada', in R. O'Driscoll (ed.), *The Celtic Consciousness*, Dublin: Dolmen, pp. 341–7.
31 Ó Riada, S. (1982), *Our Musical Heritage*, Portlaoise: The Dolmen Press, p. 80.
32 Quinn, J. (2005), *Designing Ireland: A Retrospective Exhibition of Kilkenny Design Workshops 1963–1988*, Crafts Council of Ireland, p. 3.
33 Córas Trachtála/The Irish Export Board (1961), *Design in Ireland*, Dublin, p. xi.
34 'Irish food: a push for our plates', *Irish Times*, 26 September 2009.
35 'The next supermodel: Why the world should look at the Nordic countries', *Economist*, 2 February 2013.
36 'Shoemaker Nike's fling with Harris Tweed', *BBC News*, 19 October 2004, available from: <http://news.bbc.co.uk/2/hi/business/3756896.stm>, accessed 21 April 2013.
37 Natrass, B. and Altomare, M. (1999), *The Natural Step for Business: Wealth, Ecology and The Evolutionary Corporation*, Gabriola Island, British Columbia: New Society Publishers.

38   IKEA, 'Swedish Heritage', available from: <http://www.ikea.com/
     ms/en_IE/about_ikea/the_ikea_way/swedish_heritage/index.
     html>, accessed 21 April 2013.

39   Fuchsia Brands, 'About Fuchsia Brands', available from: <http://
     www.westcorkaplaceapart.com/about-fuchsia-brands/>, accessed
     21 April 2013.

40   Mandelson, P. (2007), 'Italy and Globalisation', Speech at the Corriere
     della Sera Foundation, Milan, 19 April.

41   Heath Ceramics, 'Our Heritage', available from: <http://www.
     heathceramics.com/home/pages/discover-heath/our-story/our-
     heritage>, accessed 21 April 2013.

42   'A label of pride that pays', *New York Times*, 23 April 2009.

43   Buffet, W. (2008), *Annual Report of Berkshire Hathaway*, Berkshire
     Hathaway Inc, available from: http://www.berkshirehathaway.
     com/2008ar/2008ar.pdf, accessed 07 May 2013.

44   O'Toole, F. (2011), 'Removal of signs shows we are going wrong
     way', *Irish Times*, 21 June.

45   Weintraub, B. (1986), 'Dingle – Ireland, Country Style', *National
     Geographic Traveler*, summer, pp. 60–70.

46   'Dingle all the way', *Irish Times*, 30 November 2012.

47   See www.arabianranta.fi and www.iledenantes.com.

48   'The pride and prejudice of "local"', *New York Times*, 8 July 2010.

49   'The luck of the Irish', *Fortune Magazine*, 25 October 1999.

50   'Directors oppose axing of film board', *Irish Independent*, 22 Septem-
     ber 2009.

51   'If arts funding is abolished, where will the next Brendan Gleeson
     come from?', *Irish Independent*, 26 September 2009.

52   Bradley, J. (2007), 'Small State, Big World: Reflections on Irish
     Economic Development', *Dublin Review of Books*, No. 3, autumn.

53   O'Connor, P. (2000), *Beyond the Mist: What Irish Mythology Can Teach
     Us About Ourselves*, London: Orion.

54   'A genius departs', *Economist*, 8 October 2011.

55   Ó Tuama, S. (2008), *Aguisíní*, Baile Átha Cliath: Coiscéim.

56   United Nations World Commission on Environment and Develop-
     ment (WCED) (1987), *Our Common Future*, (The Brundtland Report),
     New York: United Nations.

57   Porter, M.E. and Kramer, M.R. (2011), 'Creating Shared Value',
     Harvard Business Review, January–February.

58   Horgan, S. (1997), *Seán Lemass: The Enigmatic Patriot*, Dublin: Gill &
     Macmillan, p. 351.

59 Fanning, J. (2011), 'Branding and Begorrah: The Importance of Ireland's Brand Image', *Irish Marketing Review*, 21(1&2), pp. 23–31.

60 Bord Bia/Irish Food Board (2012), *Understanding Irish Consumer Behaviour*, 12 June, and *Feeling the Pinch 6: The Consumer Outlook – January 2012*, both available from: <http://www.bordbia.ie/industry services/information/publications/bbreports/Pages/Marketing Reports.aspx>, accessed 07 May 2013.

61 'Foreign Affairs: The Lexus and the Shamrock', *New York Times*, 3 August 2001.

62 O'Connor, G. (2010), *To Understand Shame is to Understand Addiction and Maybe Even Life Itself*, Betty Ford Institute (BFI), Staff Publications, November 11, Rancho Mirage, CA.

63 Horgan, J. (2010), *The Song at Your Backdoor*, Cork: The Collins Press, p. 156.

64 'President inspired by Ireland's "resourcefulness"', *Irish Times*, 22 December 2011.

65 Shaw, G.B. (1921), *Back to Methuselah: A Metabiological Pentateuch*, London: Constable.

66 Whelan, K. (2011), *Atlas of the Irish Rural Landscape*, 2nd ed., Cork: Cork University Press.

Chapter 3

1 Shelman, M. (2012), 'Driving for Continuous Progress' in Bord Bia (2012), *Pathways for Growth: Building Ireland's Largest Indigenous Industry (Progress Update 3: May 2011–May 2012)*, Dublin, p. 11.

2 Lieb, D. (2012), interviewed by Finbarr Bradley, 1 March.

3 Yeats, W.B. (1961), *Essays and Introductions*, New York, p. 213.

4 Bradley, F. and Kennelly, J.J. (2008), *Capitalising on Culture, Competing on Difference: Innovation, Learning and a Sense of Place in a Globalising Ireland*, Dublin: Blackhall Publishing.

5 O'Rahilly, T. (2012), interviewed by Finbarr Bradley, 22 February.

6 'Admission: one pot of gold, to be sure and begorrah', *Sunday Tribune*, 7 February 2010.

7 'The Louvre of Leprechauns', *Irish Times*, 10 March 2010.

8 'Ireland's new museum for leprechauns', *Time Magazine*, 11 March 2010.

9 Ward, M.E. (2010), 'Marketing the Emerald Isle: a Modest Proposal', 27 May, available from: <http://margaretward.ie/2010/05/marketing-the-emerald-isle-a-modest-proposal/>, accessed 21 April 2013.

10 Cox, D. (2012), interviewed by Finbarr Bradley, 23 February.
11 Foreword by Malachy McCloskey in Carroll, K. (2005), *A Darling Little Mill: The Story of the Lifeforce Mill in Cavan*, unpublished corporate brochure, p. 3.

Chapter 4

1   'Go green', *Irish Times*, 31 May 2008.
2   'Global Vision Awards 2010', *Travel + Leisure Magazine*, New York, November, available from: <http://www.travelandleisure.com/articles/global-vision-awards-2010/3>, accessed 21 April 2013.
3   Cnoc Suain, 'About Us', available from: <http://www.cnocsuain.com/index.php?page=about-cnoc-suain>, accessed 17 June 2013.
4   Standún, D. (2012), interviewed by James Kennelly, 20 September.
5   *Ibid.*
6   'The perfect holiday at Spiddal's peaceful hill', *Irish Times*, 10 March 2007.
7   Standún D. (2012), *op. cit.*
8   *Ibid.*
9   *Ibid.*
10 Troy, C. (2012), interviewed by James Kennelly, 20 September.
11 *Ibid.*
12 'The perfect holiday at Spiddal's peaceful hill', *op. cit.*
13 Standún, D. (2012), *op. cit.*
14 *Ibid.*
15 *Ibid.*
16 *Ibid.*
17 Miska, S., quoted in Cnoc Suain, '"Folklocic" Evening – Oiche Airneáin', available from: <http://www.cnocsuain.com/index.php?page=folkloric-evening-oiche-airneain>, accessed 16 April 2013.
18 Standún, D. (2012), *op. cit.*
19 Troy, C. (2012), *op. cit.*
20 Standún, D. (2012), *op. cit.*
21 Gilmore, J.H. and Pine II, B.J. (2007), *Authenticity: What Consumers Really Want*, Boston, MA: Harvard Business School Press.

Chapter 5

1   Van Eyck (1961), 'The medicine of reciprocity tentatively reciprocated', first published in *FORUM* magazine, April–May, reprinted

in Ligtelijn, V. and Strauven, F. (eds.) (2008), *Aldo van Eyck: Collected Articles and Other Writings 1947–1988*, Amsterdam: Sun Publishers, p. 318.

2   Whelan, B. (2008), 'Globalising Irish Music' in Mathews, P.J., *UCD Scholarcast: The Art of Popular Culture*, Series 1, Scholarcast 7, and Butler, J. (2006), 'Re-Imagining Irish Dance' in Higgins Wyndham, A., *Re-Imagining Ireland*, Charlottesville: University of Virginia Press, pp. 140–4.

3   'Heritage Luxury: Past becomes the Future', *New York Times*, 8 November 2010.

4   'Why the show born with Michael Flatley's puffy shirts and leather trousers means so much to China', *Irish Times*, 25 February 2012.

5   Heaney, S. (2002), *The Redress of Poetry: Oxford Lectures*, London: Faber and Faber.

6   Ó Riada, S. (1982), *Our Musical Heritage*, Portlaoise: Dolmen.

7   Ó Súilleabháin, M. (1981), 'Irish Music Defined', *The Crane Bag*, 5(2), pp. 83–7.

8   'Heaney receives DCU's highest award', *Irish Times*, 11 May 2011.

9   Eisner, E.W. (2002), *The Arts and the Creation of Mind*, New Haven and London: Yale University Press.

10 Reed, H. (1944), *Education through Art*, New York: Pantheon Books.

11 'Building blocks in wreckage', *Irish Times*, 27 December 2010.

12 King, P. (2012), interviewed by Finbarr Bradley, 15 February.

13 'In tune and on air', *Sunday Business Post*, 13 February 2011.

14 'Philip King reflects on the cultural phenomenon that is Dingle's Other Voices', *Dingle News*, 3 December 2010, available from: <http://www.dinglenews.com/news.asp?id=4014>, accessed 28 April 2013.

15 See www.burrennationalpark.ie.

16 Dunford, B. (2011), quoted in Heritage Council, 'People and their Place: New Burren "movement" leads the way', 7 April 2011, available from: <http://www.heritagecouncil.ie/wildlife/news/view-article/article/people-and-their-place/?L=0&cHash=8618ff1929e8ed25f269 16abcb4ed7c5>, accessed 28 April 2013.

17 Hawkes-Greene, M. (2012), interviewed by Finbarr Bradley, 21 February.

18 Cummins, P. (2012), interviewed by Finbarr Bradley, 1 March.

19 *Ibid.*

20 *Ibid.*

21 *Ibid.*

22 Collins, P. (2009), 'Lights, Camera, Action: The Emergence of a Television Production Cluster on Ireland's West Coast', paper presented to

the *Irish Social Science Platform (ISSP) Annual Conference*, Whitaker Institute for Innovation and Societal Change, NUIG, Galway, 2 December.

23 Fallon, B. (1999), *An Age of Innocence: Irish Culture 1930–1960*, New York: St. Martin' Press, p. 159.

24 Garvin, T. (2004), *Preventing the Future: Why Ireland was so Poor for so Long*, Dublin: Gill & Macmillan, p. 44.

25 Germany, the strongest economy in Europe, has only 26 per cent of 25–34 year-olds with third-level qualifications, whereas the corresponding figure for Ireland is 48 per cent, the highest university participation rate in the EU. See 'Why send so many to third level?', *Irish Times*, 19 July 2012.

26 Jelski, D. (2012), 'The Three Laws of Future Employment', available from: <http://www.newgeography.com/content/002656-the-three-laws-future-employment>, accessed 28 April 2013.

Chapter 6

1   Ruskin, J. (1870), 'Lecture 3: The Relation of Art to Morals', *Lectures on Art*, New York: John Wiley & Son, section 95.

2   'Irish Craft: Celebrating the Best in Irish Design', Special Report, *Irish Times*, 9 June 2011, p. 8.

3   Mulcahy, L. (2012), interviewed by Finbarr Bradley, 6 March.

4   *Louis Mulcahy Pottery on the Dingle Peninsula, Co. Kerry, Ireland* (2009), Louis Mulcahy Pottery (video), available from: <http://www.louismulcahy.com/lmp_videos.asp>, accessed 28 April 2013.

5   de Staic, B. (2011), interviewed by James Kennelly, 2 March.

6   *Ibid.*

7   McCarthy Fisher, J. (2012), interviewed by Finbarr Bradley, 21 February.

8   DoChara, 'Irish Tweed', available from <http://www.dochara.com/tour/things-to-buy/irish-tweed/>, accessed 30 April 2013.

9   See www.molloyandsons.com.

10 *Cushendale Mills Prepares for 35th Showcase* (2010), Showcase Ireland (video), available from: <http://www.youtube.com/watch?v=2LoK5H9aMe8>, accessed 28 April 2013.

11 *Ibid.*

12 'Irish Craft: celebrating the best in Irish design', special report, *Irish Times*, 9 June 2011, p. 8.

Chapter 7

1   'Yep, it's cool to be a farmer again', *Irish Times*, 9 September 2011.
2   Downey, L. (2012), 'The Cork Butter Exchange (1770–1924): The National and International Importance and Ultimate Demise of the Enterprise', *Times Past 2012–13* (Journal of Muskerry Local History Society), 10, pp. 52–62.
3   'Joe McGough', *Sunday Independent*, 16 November 2003.
4   Lysaght, P. (2004), 'Taste Kerrygold, Experience Ireland: An Ethnological Perspective on Food Marketing', *Béaloideas*, 72, pp. 61–90.
5   *Ibid.*
6   'Food firms keen to serve up in Germany', *Irish Times*, 7 April 2012.
7   Andrews, C. (2007), 'Country Comforts', *Saveur*, 12 March.
8   *Ibid.*
9   *Ibid.*
10 *Ibid.*
11 Andrews, C. (2009), *The Country Cooking of Ireland*, San Francisco: Chronicle Books, p. 19
12 *Ibid*, p. 13.
13 'Bia, glorious bia', *Irish Times*, 13 March 2010.
14 'Jam-maker spreads the good news with expansion plans', *Irish Times*, 13 November 2012.
15 Lavery, M. (2009), 'Sweet Success', *Country Living*, 4 April, p. 6.
16 'Bord Bia event attracts 520 buyers', *Irish Times*, 8 February 2012.
17 'Food firms keen to serve up in Germany', *op. cit.*
18 *Ibid.*
19 See www.origingreen.ie.
20 Cotter, A. (2011), 'Building the Brand Reputation of Irish Food and Drink', paper presented to Bord Bia's *Food and Drink Summit*, UCD Michael Smurfit Graduate Business School, Dublin, 27 May.
21 *Ibid.*
22 'Go-ahead for Teagasc GM trials criticised', *Irish Times*, 27 July 2012.
23 'Branding has to be built on "green and unspoilt" reputation', *Irish Independent*, 17 June 2008.
24 See www.aniarrestaurant.ie.
25 'Is Guaranteed Irish still a good idea?', *Irish Times*, 10 September 2011.
26 Clancy, T. (2010), 'My Irish AC Proposal', 20 February, available from: <http://tomasclancy.wordpress.com/the-irish-ac-proposal>, accessed 28 April 2013.
27 'As Irish as tea from China', *Irish Times*, 22 November 2010.

28 McKinney, D.W. and Stirling, W.S. (1972), *Gurteen College: A Venture of Faith*, Omagh: The Strule Press, p. 7.

29 See www.feilefoods.ie.

30 Cahill, J. (2007), 'Bilingualism on Food Packaging – Researching the Potential', draft report for Foras na Gaeilge, Food Development Centre, Dublin Institute of Technology, December.

31 Hennessy, T., Kinsella, A., Moran, B. and Quinlan, G. (2011), *Teagasc National Farm Survey 2011*, available from: <http://www.teagasc. ie/publications/2012/1293/TeagascNationalFarmSurvey2011-alltables.pdf>, accessed 2 July 2013, and Bord Bia (2013), 'Food and Drink Exports Surpass €9 Billion for the First Time', press release, 9 January, available from: <http://www.bordbia.ie/eventsnews/ press/pages/PerformanceProspects2013.aspx>, accessed 2 July 2013.

32 'An awakening giant', *Irish Times*, 16 January 2012.

33 Boyle, G. (2008), 'Towards 2030: Teagasc's Role in Transforming Ireland's Agri-Food Sector and the Wider Bioeconomy', Teagasc Foresight Report, Oak Park, Carlow, May, p. 5.

34 COFORD (Council for Forest Research and Development) (2005), *Rural Ireland 2025: Foresight Projections*, Joint publication of NUI Maynooth, University College Dublin & Teagasc, available from: <http://www. coford.ie/media/coford/content/publications/projectreports/ Foresight.pdf>, accessed 2 July 2013.

35 'Venture capitalists are making bigger bets on food start-ups', *New York Times*, 28 April 2013.

36 Feehan, J. (2003), *Farming in Ireland: History, Heritage and Environment*, Faculty of Agriculture, University College Dublin, p. 525.

37 *Ibid*, p. 524.

38 Ballymaloe Cookery School, 'About the Ballymaloe Cookery School', available from: <http://www.cookingisfun.ie/pages/about_us/>, accessed 28 April 2013.

39 Norberg-Hodge, H., Merrifield, T. and Gorelick, S. (2002), *Bringing the Food Economy Home: Local Alternatives to Global Agribusiness*, London: Zed Books.

Chapter 8

1 The Dubliners, '"Finnegan's Wake" Lyrics', available from: <http:// www.golyr.de/the-dubliners/songtext-finnegan-s-wake-14585. html>, accessed 29 April 2013.

2 'A nation's stout heart', *Irish Times*, 19 September 2009.

3   'Real story of 250-year quest for the perfect pint', *Irish Times*, 25 September 2009.
4   Teeling, J. (2007), foreword to *Locke's Distillery: A History* by Andrew Bielenberg, 1993 (reissued in 2007), Dublin: The Lilliput Press.
5   Cooley Distillery, 2010 Annual Report, pp. 3–4.
6   Teeling, J. (2011), interviewed by James Kennelly, 26 August.
7   Chairman's Statement, Cooley Distillery 2010 Annual report, p. 3.
8   'The Whiskey Rush', *Innovation* (*Irish Times* monthly magazine), February 2012.
9   'Warm glow of satisfaction as whiskey firm is sold for $95m', *Irish Times*, 16 December 2011.
10 Beam Inc. (2012), 'Beam Completes Acquisition of Cooley Distillery', press release, 17 January, available from: <http://www.beamglobal.com/news/press-releases/press-releases-65>, accessed 29 April 2013.
11 *Ibid.*
12 'I'll drink to that: world's oldest distillery Cooley is sold for €73 million', *Irish Independent*, 17 December 2011.
13 'World goes Gaga for Irish whiskey', *Irish Independent*, 8 July 2012.

Chapter 9

1   Meyer, K. (1913), *Ancient Irish Poetry*, London: Constable, reproduced in Heaney, S. (1980), 'The God in the Tree: Early Irish Nature Poetry', *Preoccupations: Selected Prose 1968–1978*, London: Faber & Faber, pp. 181–9.
2   Shrivastava, P. and Kennelly, J.J. (2013), 'Sustainability and Place-Based Enterprise', *Organization & Environment*, 26(1), pp. 83–101.
3   Bord na Móna, 'Policy on Peat & Peatlands', available from <http://www.bordnamona.ie/our-company/sustainability/policy-on-peat-and-peatlands/>, accessed 5 July 2013.
4   Glen Dimplex, 'The Glen Dimplex Group', available from <http://www.glendimplex.com>, accessed 2 July 2013.
5   Kingspan, 'Key Financial: Financial Highlights', available from <http://www.kingspan.com/investors/key-financial.aspx>, accessed 18 June 2013.
6   Shrivastava, P. and Kennelly, J.J., *op. cit.*
7   *Building Successful Businesses* (2013), Glen Dimplex Group (video), available from: <http://www.glendimplex.com/our_story>, accessed 1 May 2013.

8   Kennelly, J.J. (2001), *The Kerry Way: The History of the Kerry Group*, Dublin: Oak Tree Press, p. 52.

9   Kerry Group plc, 'Share Price Information', available from: <http://www.kerrygroup.com/page.asp?pid=122> and <http://www.kerrygroup.com/page.asp?pid=120>, accessed 25 May 2013.

10   Kennelly, J.J. (2001), *op. cit.*, p. 251.

11   'Major Endeavour changes include global investor showcase', *Endeavour News*, Q1 2011, Issue 1, p. 3, available from: <http://www.endeavour.biz/images/EndeavourNewsQ12011.pdf>, accessed 29 April 2013.

12   Translation: 'yes, we can!'

13   Kinmonth, C. (2009), 'Past, Present, Future: Irish vernacular furniture as inspiration', paper presented to *The Presence of the Past: Influences on Contemporary Irish Furniture Design* conference, GMIT, Letterfrack, County Galway, 22–23 October, pp. 55–64.

14   Walton, M. (2012), interviewed by Finbarr Bradley, 28 February.

15   VOYA, 'VOYA Story', available from: <http://www.voya.ie/voya-story/>, accessed 29 April 2013.

16   Walton, M. (2011), 'VOYA: Organic Beauty from the Sea', paper presented to the *Bord Bia Brand Forum Event*, Tayto Park, Ashbourne, County Meath, 13 September, available from: <http://www.bordbia.ie/industryservices/brandforum/events/Documents/Mark%20Walton%20-%20Voya.pdf>, accessed 18 April 2013.

17   Rockstrom, J., Steffen, W., Noone, K., Persson, A., Chapin III, F.S., Lambin, E.F. and Foley, J.A. (2009), 'Safe operating space for humanity', *Nature*, 461, pp. 472–5.

18   EPA (2013), 'Projections show Ireland will not meet its EU Greenhouse Gas emissions targets', press release, 25 April, available from: <http://www.epa.ie/newsandevents/news/name,51811,en.html>, accessed 2 July 2013.

19   Government of Ireland (2012), *Action Plan for Jobs*, Dublin: Government Publications, p. 78.

20   Brennan, P. (2012), *Ireland's Green Opportunity: Driving Investment in a Low-Carbon Economy* (ebook), Dublin: Orpen Press.

Chapter 10

1   Lenihan, D. (2010), *The Path to Freedom: Speeches by Michael Collins*, Dublin: Original Writing, p. 93.

Endnotes

2   'Irish president urges ECB reform or risk social upheaval', *Financial Times*, 1 May 2013.

3   Higgins, M.D. (2011), *Renewing the Republic*, Dublin: Liberties Press.

4   Higgins, M.D. 'Of Public Intellectuals, Universities, and a Democratic Crisis, available from: <http://www.president.ie/speeches/of-public-intellectuals-universities-and-a-democratic-crisis/>, accessed 1 May 2013.

5   Ricoeur, P. (1961), 'Universal Civilization and National Cultures', in Kelbley, C.A. (1965), *History and Truth*, Evanston: Northwestern University Press, pp. 276–7.

6   Horgan, J. (1997), *Seán Lemass: The Enigmatic Patriot*, Dublin: Gill & Macmillan.

7   FitzGerald, G. (1964), 'Seeking a National Purpose', *Studies*, Winter, pp. 337–51.

8   Keating, J., quoted in Shaw-Smith, D. (2003), *Traditional Crafts of Ireland*, revised ed., London: Thames & Hudson, p. 9.

9   'The challenges we face demand a comprehensive vision of the sort of society we want to see emerge', *Irish Times*, 24 August 2009.

10 'Ireland will suffer without investment', *Irish Times*, 29 November 2011.

11 Lenihan, D. (2010), *op cit.*, pp. 88–9.

12 'State now morally as well as economically bankrupt', *Irish Times*, 26 March 2012.

13 Feehan, J. (2003), *Farming in Ireland: History, Heritage and Environment*, Faculty of Agriculture, University College Dublin, p. 526.

Index